ALSO BY CONSTANCE SANTEGO

FICTION
(Novels are based on actual events)
The Nine Spiritual Gifts Series:
Journey of a Soul

NONFICTION
Fairy Tales, Dreams and Reality... Where Are You On Your Path? Second Edition

Your Persona... The Mask You Wear

Angelic Lifestyle, A Vibrant Lifestyle &
Angelic Lifestyle's 42-Day Energy Cleanse

Archangel Michael's Soul Retrieval Guide

SECRETS OF A HEALER, SERIES:
Magic Of Aromatherapy (Vol I)
Magic Of Reflexology (Vol II)
Magic Of The Gifts (Vol III)
Magic Of Muscle Testing (Vol IV)
Magic Of Iridology (Vol V)
Magic Of Massage (Vol VI)
Magic Of Hypnotherapy (Vol VII)
Magic Of Reiki (Vol VIII)

Intuitive Life – The Gift of Prophecy, third edition
Copyright © 2020 by Constance Santego.
Original copywrite © 2007 The Intuitive Life, A Guide to Self-Knowledge & Healing through Psychic Development under Connie Brummet

All rights reserved. No part of this publication may be reproduced, distributed or transmitted in any form or by any means, including photocopying, recording, or other electronic or mechanical methods, without the prior written permission of the publisher, except in the case of brief quotations embodied in critical reviews and certain other noncommercial uses permitted by copyright law. For permission requests, write to the publisher, addressed "Attention: Permissions Coordinator," at the address below.

Copy Editor & Interior Design: Constance Santego
Book Layout: ©2017 BookDesignTemplates.com
Cover Design: Jennifer Louie

Ordering Information:
Quantity sales. Special discounts are available on quantity purchases by corporations, associations, and others. For details, contact the "Special Sales Department" at the address above.

Trade paperback ISBN: 978-1-7770818-8-1

eBook ISBN 978-1-7770818-9-8

Created and published In Canada. Printed and bound in the United States of America

Third Edition
Published by Maximillian Enterprises
Kelowna, BC
Canada
www.constancesantego.ca

INTUITIVE LIFE
THE GIFT OF PROPHECY

THIRD EDITION

Constance Santego

Maximillian Enterprises
Kelowna, BC

Dedication

To Spirit, thanks for always giving me inspiration, motivation, and an opportunity for transformation.

I am so

Happy and Grateful now that I am open to receiving infinite blessings from the universe into my life.

Affirmations are a type of talisman, and when you repeat something three times (3x) your mind has time to comprehend what you have said and takes note that it is an important message to you.

Contents

Preface xiv
Note to Reader xix
Learning Outcome xxi
The Nine Spiritual Gifts xxiii
Introduction 1
Section One 4
      Energy 4
      Light Energy 7
      Vibration, Frequency & Spiritual Energy 10
Electromagnetic Vibration 14
      Human Body 14
      Nutrition and Exercise 14
Physical Vibration 15
      Kirlian Photography 15
      Vital Field (Aura) 16
      Layers of the Aura 19
      Colors of the Aura 25
      Meanings of the Auric Colors 26
      Aura Overview 30
      The Most Famous Proof of Auras 31
      Chakras 32
      Meridians 33
Astral-Etheric Vibration 34
      Raising Your Vibratory Rate 35
      Breath 36
      Thought Energy 37
Section Two Learning To Listen 39
      GETTING ANSWERS 39

Exercise #1 – *Visual* – Complimentary Colors 41
Exercise #2 – *Visual* – Aura 42
Exercise #3 – *Visual* – Intuitive Art 44
Exercise #4 – *Visual* – Practice Your Intuition 46
Exercise #5 – *Feeler* – Breath A 48
Exercise #6 – *Feeler* – Breath B 49
Exercise #7 – *Feeler* – Pendulum 51
Exercise #8 – *Feeler* – Body Pendulum 58
Exercise #9 – *Audio* – Automatic Writing 60
Exercise #10 – *Knower* – Thought Energy A 61
Exercise #11 – *Knower* – Thought Energy B 62
Exercise #12 – *Knower* – Psychometry 63
Astral Projection 67
Exercise #13 – *Knower & Visual* – Remote Viewing 69
Exercise #14 – *Knower & Feeler* – Body Scan 71
Exercise #15 – *Knower, Visual, Audio & Feeler* – Animal Sensing 74
Exercise #16 – *Audio, Feeler, Knower & Visual* – Psychic Detective 76

Section Three Prophecy Psychic Readings 78
SYMBOLISM 83
Tea Leaf Reading 85
PROPHECY READINGS 86
Reading Exercise #1 - For A Lost Items 86
Reading Exercise #1 - Using Automatic Writing 86
Reading Exercise #3 - Using A Pendulum 87
Reading Exercise #4 - Using Remote Viewing 87
Reading Exercise #5 - Using Sci Scan or Body Scan 88
Reading Exercise #6 - Using Astral Travel 88
PROPHECY SESSIONS 89

- Reading Exercise #7 - Using Your Psychic Energy 89
- Reading Exercise #8 - Using A Telephone or The Internet 92
- Reading Exercise #9 - Using Psychometry 92
- Reading Exercise #10 - Using Aura Art 92
- Reading Exercise #11 - Using Tarot Card 93
  - Numbers 97
  - Time 99
  - Reading the Cards 100
  - The Deck - The High/Major Arcana 101
  - The Low/ Minor Arcana 116
  - Wands = Clubs 117
  - Cups = Hearts 121
  - Swords = Spades 125
  - Pentacles = Diamonds 130
  - The Game of Tarot 135
  - Tarot Card Reading Arrangements 137
- Reading Exercise #12 - Astrology 141
  - The Chart 149
  - Basic Chart / Aries Chart 162
  - Phases of the Moon 166
  - Zodiac Signs 187
  - Planets 203
  - Aspects / Angles: 208
  - Patterns 211
  - Astrology Charting Procedure 215
- Bibliography - Appendices 225
  - Appendix I: A Suggested Reading List 225
  - Appendix II: A Suggested Internet Resources 232
  - Appendix III: A Suggested Video Resources 235

Appendix IV: A Glossary of Common Terms............237

Preface

Gift of Prophecy

So how did I get to now?

I now believe that my childhood made me strong and determined to find a better way of life.

I was born into a childhood romance; my mother, small and pregnant, was married in pink when she was sixteen years old. My father who was three years older was a dreamer, always trying to be something or someone he was not - a miner, a traveling salesman, but never knowing a real job...

We lived in nineteen different homes in four different towns by the time I reached eight years of age. Memories of those precious years are terrible. Yelling, spanking, crying, and being scared is what I remember most - happy during the day and walking on eggshells as soon as my Dad arrived home at night.

My mother did her best looking after my sister and I in trailers or one-bedroom basement suits, with minimal furniture and food. Hand-me-down clothes, struggling to keep up with my education due to all the different schools I attended, never knowing how long this new friend was going to be with me, were some of my life lessons.

From the age of ten I helped my divorced mom (thank God!) with her businesses and by mid-twenties I owned my first business - an awning and canvas repair business...just like Mom.

When I was twenty-nine, I had to sell my business, due to the excruciating pain in my lower back that would cause me to collapse onto the floor. Not wanting an operation, I investigated alternative healing for relief of the pain. I went to a few different practitioners who practiced: chiropractic, massage, emotional clearing, reflexology, and muscle testing to name a few - and they all helped heal my back. I then studied many of these courses, and at the age of thirty-one was working in an alternative health clinic.

Interesting how life's many twists and turns, ups and downs are blessings in disguise. One day life is mundane and the next it is magical.

I believe that we all have a purpose on Earth, that we are granted time to experience and learn what is necessary for each of us. I know that I want to help people in a big way—not just a small way. I had a practitioner muscle test me once on how times I have been down here on Earth, many times, over ten thousand times. Why, you might ask, why do I keep coming back? I think it is because I have a great ability to help the human spirit. I could move on, change my frequency in the level of light and stay there but I have found that spirits there work harder than I do here. Also, human beings do not seem to understand that these spirits are trying to help and communicate with us. Most people are scared when something unusual happens and many are put on medication. So, I find that I can help more here than if I stayed up there.

My dream is to witness the new era, where there is no war, only peace on Earth, when all people are respected equally, and our purpose of this lifetime will be apparent to all. Man will be in control of his own life; self-empowerment, self-love, and humanity will be the goal. There will be no judgment, just the understanding that everyone is on an individual path of enlightenment and that we all are at different stages in our development. Each of us needs different experiences to gain the wisdom required for the new millennium and the afterlife.

Heaven on Earth is to know that we each create our own future; every thought, decision and action creates a wave of reality that makes that determination. We make our choices freely with no one to blame but ourselves.

Every waking moment is a new opportunity to change your mind and choose a different route. You are the only one who can take control of your life and go forward to build a better tomorrow.

In this manual, I will share with you; knowledge, stories, and inspirations about psychic healing *emotionally, spiritually, mentally* and *physically,* for I have not seen that we can do that in the afterlife. I urge you to enjoy the precious time you have with your loved ones…to teach and learn from your children and finally… to be careful what you think, day dream, say and do for you create your own future. Your journey on Earth takes such a short time, a metaphoric blink of an eye, compared with the afterlife.

May you go forward in love and light, with wisdom and self-empowerment.

Enjoy your Journey, Constance

Note to Reader

This handbook is not to replace a medical doctor or other professionals. It is a course that I teach on how to develop your intuition and psychic abilities.

Every book I have written is based on one of the nine spiritual gifts and to understand all that I am teaching, my suggestion to you is to read all my manuals and novels.

Shift happens...Create magic!

Learning Outcome

When you have completed this book and studied the concepts and techniques, you:

- know and understand the sources of energy
- know and understand Your Vital Field (Aura)
- the spiritual importance of Breath, Nutrition, and Exercise
- Learn many unique techniques for finding answers to yours and other people's questions
- be able to interpret symbolism and do "prophecies" for yourself and others

This manual is part of the 'Intuitive Life Course' that Connie teaches to her students, all stories are from her experiences. Enjoy!

The Nine Spiritual Gifts

In the New Testament, my favorite story is "The Gifts".
(Corinthians 1, Chapter 12, Verse 4-11)
(Maybe a little differently worded depending on which Bible you have).

The variety and the unity of gifts
There are many different gifts, but it is always the same Spirit; there are many different ways of serving, but it is always the same Lord. There are many different forms of activity, but in everybody, it is the same God who is at work in them all. The particular manifestation of the Spirit granted to each one is to be used for the general good. To one is given from the Spirit the gift of utterance expressing **wisdom**; to another the gift of utterance expressing **knowledge**; in accordance with the same Spirit to another, **faith**, from the same Spirit; and to another, the gifts of **healing**, through the same Spirit; to another, the working of **miracles**; to another **prophecy**; to another, the power of **distinguishing spirits**; to one, the gift of **different tongues** and to another, the **interpretation of tongues**. But at work in all these is one and the same Spirit, distributing them at will to each individual.

The New Jerusalem Bible

Intuitive Life

THIRD EDITION

Introduction

The Gift of Prophecy - Most people, when they hear the word 'prophecy,' the first thing they think of is a prediction of something to come, a fortuneteller, or something of that nature.

In the Bible (Deuteronomy 18, 10-11), it says not to go to a soothsayer, augur or sorcerer, weaver of spells, consulter of ghosts or mediums, or necromancer, meaning. . . fortune-tellers.

In my thirties, I prayed up to God to ask why.

The answer I received back down was, let us say a person comes to see you, and you tell them their future, and it comes true. Three months, six months, a year later, they come back and want you to do it again, and again it comes true. Now you have created a co-dependent person that needs you to tell them how to live their life.

I asked back up, "So what do I do with this gift I have?"

The answer that came back down was 'teach.' Teach people how to be in control of their own lives. And so that is what I do, teach.

In this book, you are going to find four different ways that I teach my students to sense energy; Visually (visual), Audibly (audio), Kinesthetically (feeler), and through thought (knower).

If you cannot interpret the information, then you are never going to be able to prophecies.

Constance Santego

Section One

Energy

The Gift of Prophecy is more than telling the future. It is interpreting and intentionally influencing energy. You use energy every day, to eat, to play, to work, to pray, and to sleep. Even a small child uses energy, when he or she jumps on a trampoline, slides down a slide, swings, yells making happy or sad sounds. Energy is all around us, and we manipulate it constantly.

So why are people afraid of their intuition? It is just energy. What if you thought of intuition as a highly acute sense of energy your subtle body could decode or decipher?

Think of your intuition or extrasensory perception as a cell phone. Imagine that you are making a phone call, pretend you are calling a person in, let us say, Japan. You dialed their number, and moments later, you are talking to the person. Nowadays, most people do not even blink an eye at the enormous amount of energy being manipulated to call this person in Japan.

Think about everything that must happen from the moment you thought about making that call. First, you had to think about calling. Then you went and found your phone, picked it up, and dialed the number even before you talked.

But there is more to it than even all that!

The mechanism inside your phone changed your voice into electricity and transmitted the sound wave (cellular wave) of energy from your cell phone and broadcasted it to one or more towers (Earth) which transferred the cellular wave into radio waves or microwaves to many satellites (which are traveling out in space, hovering beyond our atmosphere, somewhere between Earth and the moon).

Then the wave is transmitted from the satellite back to Earth ... and the receiving cell phone or telephone in Japan (then the waves travel back and forth as you speak). Not to mention that it is a manipulation of energy, it is done at supersonic speed.

You cannot see, taste, hear, or smell radio, micro, or cellular waves, and most of us obviously cannot feel them, but they exist. The cellular wave or vibration of information is being transmitted and then decoded and deciphered by the receiver.

What if?

Intuitive energy was the same; it is! Intuitive energy transmits and receives (sensing/reading) a vibration. It is a frequency spectrum of energy coming from a person, place, or thing that is decoded and interpreted by you.

In the Bible, this energy is one of the nine Spiritual Gifts...called Tongues. And this type of energy is quantum quick... quicker than a photon, a single quantum of light *(or of any other form of electromagnetic radiation)*.

Light Energy

I know, now you need to understand what energy is?

The dictionary's definition of energy is:

- ✓ forcefulness and vigor in actions or words,
- ✓ busy activity, to devote one's energies to making a success of an enterprise,
- ✓ the unifying concept of all physical science that associates with any system,
- ✓ a capacity for work either because of the motion of the mass in the system (kinetic energy),
- ✓ the configuration of masses or charges in the system (potential energy)
- ✓ or the presence of photons in the system (radiant energy).

Energy is a scalar quantity with dimensions that possesses the properties of mass according to the theory of relativity, assigning to a M, an energy such that $C2$ = M where E is the energy and C2 is the speed of light.

<u>mass x length 2</u>

time

The most famous scientific equation of energy is $E=Mc2$. This formula implies that even an everyday object at rest with a modest amount of mass has an exceptionally large amount of energy. Basically, energy is the ability to make things move.

Did you know that there are ten kinds of energy, Magnetic, Electrical, Sound, Gravitational, Elastic, Light, Thermal, Mechanical, Chemical, and Nuclear?

The categories of energy are divided into three groups:

Potential	Kinetic	Radiation
Stored energy or energy related to position	*Energy of motion*	*Energy without particles*
Elastic	Mechanical	Light
Nuclear	Thermal	*Intuition?*
Magnetic	Electrical	
Gravitational	Sound	
Chemical		

In this book, you will be learning how to work with *light* energy (energy without particles). You may not necessarily be able to sense that you are doing anything, though it will be happening, just as in the examples below.

- ✓ Ultraviolet light and infra-red light are undetectable by the human eye.
- ✓ Dogs can hear sounds that we cannot hear.
- ✓ Animals' sense of smell is also amazing compared to ours.

I know many of you are thinking that I am crazy to believe that intuition or ESP is provable. But at one point in history, humans couldn't accept the telephone, let alone a cordless one, and how about T.Vs., airplanes, traveling to the moon, that the Earth was round, or both men and women have the exact same number of ribs.

Times have proven that more and more is possible. Take the fastest man; records are being broken daily. The smallest thing was the atom… and now it is a quark… tomorrow it will be? In Russia, 100's of miles underground, are laboratories where scientists are studying particles. What will they discover next?

I hope it is that intuition is proof that intuition is a type of light energy that radiates out and into us.

Don't worry; the proof is coming.

Vibration, Frequency & Spiritual Energy

Why is this scientific information so important?
Because you need to raise your vibratory rate to interpret the Spiritual (intuitive or celestial) energy.

Vibration Definition
- ✓ A periodic motion of the particles of an elastic body or medium in alternately opposite directions from the position of equilibrium when that equilibrium has been disturbed (as when a stretched cord produces musical tones or molecules in the air transmit sounds to the ear).
- ✓ A characteristic emanation, aura, or spirit that infuses or vitalizes someone or something and that can be instinctively sensed or experienced —often used in plural
- ✓ A distinctive usually emotional atmosphere capable of being sensed —usually used in plural

Frequency Definition
- ✓ Frequency is the number of occurrences of a repeating event per unit of time.
- ✓ Frequency is measured in units of hertz (Hz), which is equal to one occurrence of a repeating event per second.

Frequency Example:
Sound is a traveling longitudinal wave, which is an oscillation of pressure. Humans perceive the frequency of sound waves as pitch. The notes creating music correspond to individual frequencies, which can be measured in hertz (piano, guitar, drums, etc.). The average adult human can hear sounds between 20 Hz and 16,000 Hz. The range you cannot hear is ultrasound, infrasound, and other physical vibrations such as molecular and atomic vibrations.

Frequency plays an important role in the creation of the Universe because frequency allows energy to express itself into any form, including particles, atoms, planets, stars, galaxies, and biological life. To be more specific, every biological or non-biological thing has a unique energy signature that vibrates at certain specific frequencies. Everything you can see, and touch is composed of bonded atoms that make up molecules, and all molecules have a unique vibratory rate of energy.

Think about a metal object, perhaps a metal chair. The point is, the molecules are larger, they are extremely close together and they move or vibrate very slowly. We 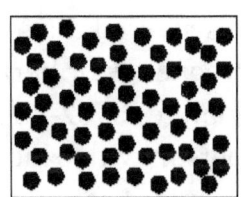 cannot see the individual molecules, but we can feel how solid and strong the metal chair is.

Now think about air. We can feel the air on a windy day. But can we see it? Perhaps we can imagine that we see air through a window, when the sunshine is hitting it and the dust 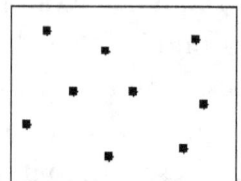 particles are now visible, or sometimes in a dust storm we think we see air moving. The point is that the air molecules are smaller, they are not close together like the metal molecules and they vibrate amazingly fast, which is why we can walk through them.

The human body is made up of trillions of cells, and each of these individual cells are made of molecules. There is no way that the human eye can detect these microscopic cells, we cannot feel each individual cell either. But a scientist can look through a microscope at our cellular structure and guess what they find? That the cells do not touch but are in fact vibrating. We only imagine we see and feel a solid mass that makes up our human body.

There are scientists, like the late Dr. Valerie Hunt, who discovered that our bodies have a specific healthy body frequency or hertz (vibration). A healthy human body vibrates at 62-78 MHz (megahertz). She found that a person with cancer has half the vibratory rate of an average healthy person. And if you raised the person's vibratory rate to a higher energy level, that person could heal (if they choose to).

- ✓ The **hertz** is a measurement of frequency, like centimeters & inches are to distance.

- ✓ It is named for Heinrich Rudolf Hertz, the first person to provide conclusive proof of the existence of electromagnetic waves.
- ✓ The term Hertz is used when it is under a 1000 cycles per second.

Spiritual Energy Definition
- ✓ Spiritual (intuition or ESP) Energy is another type of light frequency that is usually undetectable by the human sensory system.
- ✓ It is minuscule, exceptionally fast and the particles are extremely far apart (faster and further apart than air).

There are three scientific levels of frequency that we will be manipulating when using Spiritual energy:
1. **Electromagnetic vibration** (the Earth's polarity of north and south) which is what our bodies function on.
2. **Physical vibration**, this comprises auras and the energy of what is around us (other people, machines, etc.),
3. **Astral- etheric vibration** which is energy from God/Creator/Spirit.

Electromagnetic Vibration

Human Body

Human Body:
Physical   - Anatomy & Physiology Body Systems
Emotional - Chemical, Endocrine & Limbic System
Mental   - Brain & Mind
Spiritual   - Soul

Nutrition and Exercise

SPECIAL NOTE: To function intuitively, your body will require more fat to burn for the brain to be able interpret the celestial information.

- ✓ Exercise and proper nutrition will help to control your sugar cravings and excess weight gain.
- ✓ Drink enough water to flush the system.
- ✓ Eat a <u>little</u> more protein to ground yourself and help to burn the sugar.
- ✓ Think positively and breathe.

(For more information on Nutrition & Exercise, read my Angelic Lifestyle Books)

Physical Vibration

Kirlian Photography

In 1939, Semyon Kirlian discovered by accident the spiritual aura or "life force" which allegedly surrounds each living thing. What he discovered was a quite natural

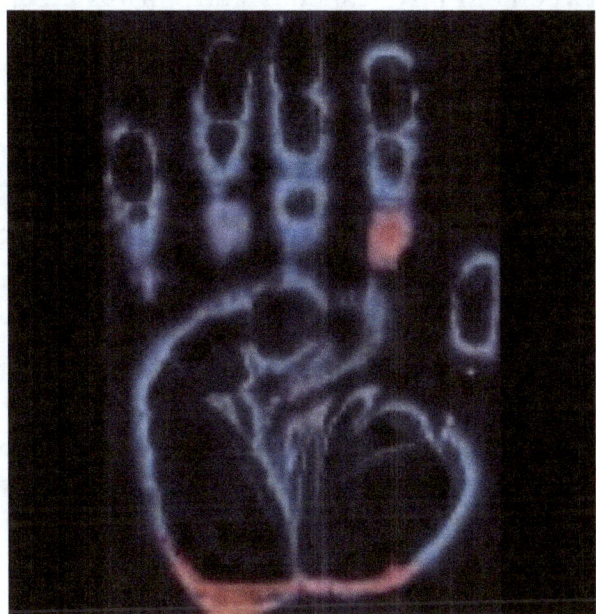

phenomena such as pressure, electrical grounding, humidity, and temperature. Changes in moisture (which may reflect changes in emotions), barometric pressure, and voltage, among other things, will produce different 'auras'.

Vital Field (Aura)

In the Native American traditions, the aura was in the legend of the white buffalo.

Descriptions in the Bible illustrate the transfiguration of Christ using colors such as white and gold.

Also known as auric field, energy field and vital body. It is the bridge between our physical body and spiritual (bliss) body.

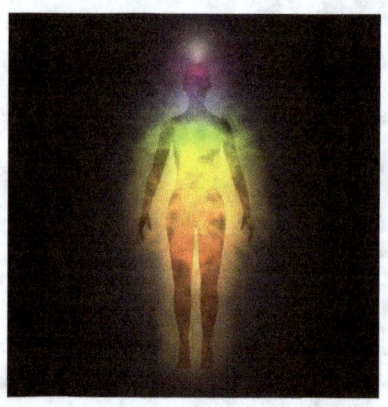

Scientists are beginning to discover forces that do not fit into the conventional Newtonian science of reality. Various researchers who recognize the vital importance and correlation of these to physical living systems are studying energies of the life-force.

Newtonian belief: The human body is seen as a cellular mechanism.

New belief: The human body is seen as Quantum energy. A new breed of physician and healer is evolving to understand the functioning of human beings, of matter, as energy. These spiritual scientists are looking to the human body as the inner workings of nature and the secrets of the universe. By realizing that human beings are energy, one can comprehend new ways of looking at health and illness. In conjunction with drug and surgical approaches, vibrational medicine attempts to treat people with pure energy. Infinity of energy is the "beyond" or the quantum outlook for the future of man. Energy work changes unhealthy conditions in the human energy system, promoting a healthy energy field and producing harmony and balance. In this balanced state, a human becomes more conscious of "self" and the connectedness of the whole and can radiate energy from all his centers of power and consciousness (chakras).

Central to the work of psycho-spiritual integration (massage. healing) is the concept that the physical body is the outward manifestation of thought patterns (many from childhood), fears and traumas that we have allowed to penetrate our energy fields. Within specific locations of our energy systems are sensations, emotions, thoughts, memories, and other non-physical experiences which we report to our doctors and therapists. Understanding how our physical symptoms are related to these locations will help us understand the nature of illness (dis-ease).

Each of our thoughts, emotions and actions can be viewed as an energy discharge radiating from a localized source into the universal field. Our personal energy field or "self" as well as everyone else's personal energy field resides and receives nourishment from this universal field. That is why on the inner levels we are all connected to one another.

Basically, the aura is the protective energy bubble that surrounds and hugs us, filtering internal, external, and environmental information. The aura or vital body delivers information to our chakras which forwards the information to our meridian system, which transports the info to our nervous system. With this information our physical, emotional, and mental body can shift as need be.

What does the auric field or vital field have to do with intuition? The vibration of energy, human or celestial, must come through our field first. Our field is the receiver for interpreting the energy.

In Quantum Medicine the aura is considered the Vital Field or Vital Body.

Layers of the Aura

The difference between an auric layer and an auric body is this: "An auric body is a body of consciousness and awareness. An Auric Layer is the representation of the chakra interacting in the aura" *Stephen Bishop*

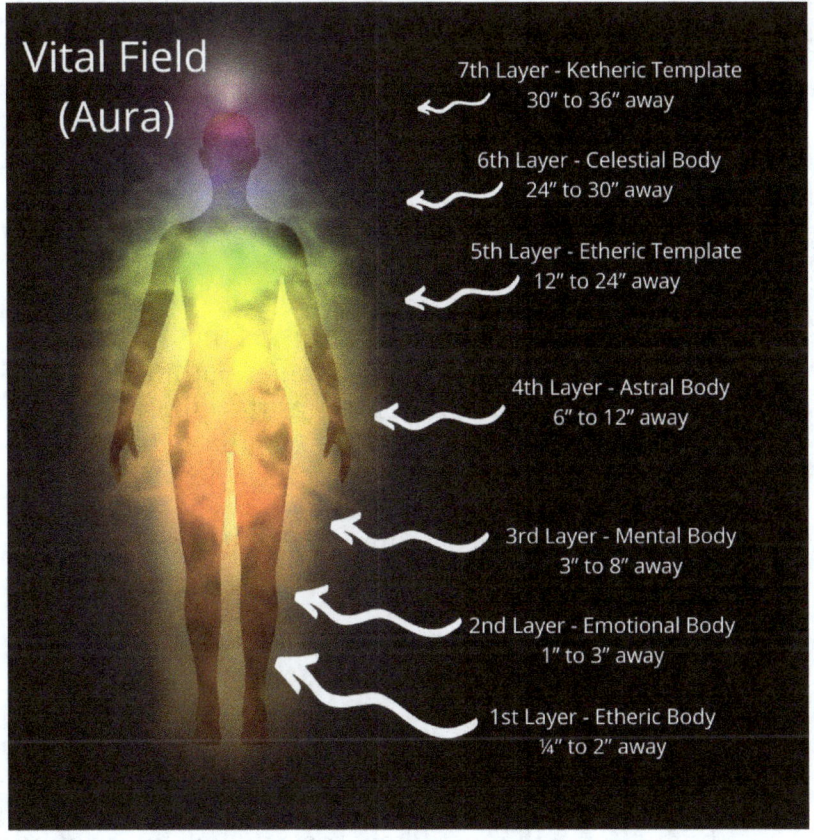

Physical Layers

1st Layer – The Etheric Body

'Ether,' the state between energy and matter (outside of our body) and our physical body (in its energy form). This layer is the closest to the real physical body and fits like a second skin (extending from a ¼" to 2" away). Most people find this layer the easiest to see, it looks like a glowing whitish/blue or grey/silver blue light.

Relates to, physical attributes, life's necessities: survival and family.

(**Ether** definition is - the rarefied element formerly believed to fill the upper regions of space).

2nd Layer – The Emotional Body

The feeling layer, which expresses the full spectrum of our emotions. Similar outline of the physical body, not as defined as the etheric body, this structure is more fluid (extending 1" to 3" from the body).

Relates to, feelings, boundaries, and creativity.

3rd Layer – The Mental Body

Structure of our ideas and thoughts, can be seen in this field. This section extends 3" to 8" from the real body and on the outside of the emotional body. You will most likely see a yellow hue around the body, particularly around the head and shoulders.

Relates to, thoughts (conscious and unconscious), beliefs, reason, and ideas.

Astral Layer

4th Layer – The Astral Body

Connection or doorway to the higher dimensions of reality. If you can astral travel, you will use this section to reach your destination. This section extends 6" to 12" from the body and connects the physical layers with the spiritual layers.

Relates to, love, and connection between mind, body, and soul.

Spiritual Layers

5th Layer – The Etheric (body's) Template

This layer contains all the body's (1st – 4th) that exist on the physical plane (layer) but in a blueprint or template form. In this layer you can change the pattern to change the dis-ease. This section extends out 12" to 24" from the body. This level is where sound transforms matter. You might see a cobalt blue color.

Relates to, the blueprint of the physical body. In this layer you will notice the pattern or template of the body's plan or design (past, present of future)

6th Layer – The Celestial Body

Some call it 'spiritual ecstasy,' where we can learn unconditional love. This section extends 24" to 30" from the body.

Relates to, enlightenment, unconditional love, group consciousness, intuition, and manifestation.

7th Layer – The Ketheric Template

Also known as Casual Body. The Ketheric template holds your present life's plan, all the auric bodies associated with the present incarnation an individual is undergoing. This section extends 30" to 36" from the body. All the chakras and auric body's forms appear to be made of golden light at this level.

Relates to, Divine, Godly, universal consciousness, life's purpose or divine plan, all aspects of the soul's experiences and access the Akashic records and past lives.

Auric Layers

Another way to envision the layers is to imagine you are building a house.

And your new home is the *Celestial Body*. You *(are the Astral Body- your connection)* hire a contractor *(who is the Ketheric Template - God/Spirit/Creator)* who hires an architect to draw the plans of the house *(Etheric Template -the blueprints)*. The Contractor then hires workers (carpenters, plumbers, electricians) and such to do the physical work *(Physical - Etheric, Emotional & Mental bodies)*.

Contractor = Ketheric Template (God)
House = Celestial Body (Your Soul)
House Plans = Etheric Template (Blueprint-Life Plan)
You = Astral Body (Connection to Your Physical Body)
Workers = All Three Physical Bodies (How you accomplish your life's plan)

All layers are important, you need all of them. The only layer we cannot change is our Ketheric Template. This is the one we were born with, God's plan for you. Karma some call it. But…we can change our Etheric Template; this is just a blueprint. The Etheric Template dictates our Physical Auric Bodies (Etheric, Emotional and Mental) which control our human physical body (anatomy, feelings, and thoughts).

Colors of the Aura

There is a difference between seeing Chakra colors (like paint) and Auric colors (like light). When you mix all the colors of light together you get white and when you mix all the colors of paint together you get black.

Facts
- ✓ The colors of a person's Auric field are telling us the person's emotional state.
- ✓ If the field is negative or clouded, we can help clear it and with the client's permission to change it to a better one.

Depending where you see the color (which auric layer) will create a bit of a difference to the meaning of the colors.

Example:
- ✓ If you see yellow within the first two inches from the body = the person is consciously thinking.
- ✓ If you see yellow three inches away from the body = the person is emotionally thinking.
- ✓ If you see yellow eight inches away from the body = the person is trying to figure something out.
- ✓ If you see yellow twelve inches away from the body = the person has left their body and is analyzing what they are seeing.
- ✓ If you see yellow twenty inches away from the body = the person is enlightened.
- ✓ If you see yellow over thirty inches away from the body = the person is communicating to Spirit.

Meanings of the Auric Colors

Black: Negative Thoughts, Power, or Education
Also- discord, hate, sometimes of great sickness, of emotional disturbance or otherwise. Universally the color of death, grief & patience. Color worn for power & authority. A color that denies light & those who wear it reject the light in themselves.

Blue: Emotional
Also -sense of wellbeing, soft, gentle, peaceful by nature, passive & introverted, value truth & honesty, trustworthy, reliable & faithful, too self-absorbed, like order in life & structure, artistic, creative, loyal, sincere. They fall in love 100%. Music helps soothe their emotions. They are harmonious, imaginative, daydream, serene and tactful.

Brown: Friendly
Also - Color of power, great energy, and the logical and analytical, self-starters. Usually moneymakers and can be very impatient too, Earthy and stability, grounded, authority, inner confidence & self-assured. Highly dedicated & committed to their family, work, & friends, practical & materialistic in life, organized & steadfast, likes to get to the root of things, no–nonsense people.

Green: Healing
Also - needs to communicate, needs a lot of affection. Very independent, thoughtful, adaptable, growth oriented, neither dominating nor submissive, extrovert

nor introvert. Seeks balance, neat and tidy at home, likes parks, coasts & open spaces. Enjoys things made from wood, clay & stone. Likes to surround themselves with plants & flowers. A lot of self-control, sympathy and likes sharing.

Magenta: Regal
Also - kindness, gentleness, consideration, affectionate, warm, compassionate, love for others, very mature with deep understanding of life, encourages others towards their full potential, co-operative, friendly, genuine, often involved in caring field, such as counseling, nursing or social work, unconditional love & affection is a typical quality

Grey: Ancient Knowledge
Also - color of fear and depression as well as unused potential. A balance between white & black. It reflects caution and is experienced as a dull and somber energy.

Orange: Action & Creative
Also - the energy of the sun. They are open-minded, emotional, and sensuous. They would rather "rule than serve". In a group they mix well. Enthusiastic, buoyant, ebullient nature, enjoy living, joyful, generally excitable, happy disposition, spontaneity & cheerfulness, talkative, outgoing, sociable, and warmhearted

Purple: Intuitive
Extremely sensitive, non-judgmental, seekers. These people have a sense of Unity (love, intellect, faith).

Red: **Go, Go, Go**
Also - energizing, vitalizing, heating, passion, material generosity, vigor, force, grounded, highly competitive, initiator, pioneer, and creator, outgoing and assertive.

Silver: **Calm & Trustworthy**
Also - lovers of convention and formality. Enjoy challenging work.

Turquoise: Tranquil
Also - unfulfilled ambitions or spiritually protected. Basically, sparkling youthfulness & bring imagination & fresh ideas to most situations, attitude of "take it in stride", decisions are made quickly & act with clarity, have a great deal of insight & talent to further spiritual path, needs to be more grounded.

Violet: Spiritual
Also - consciousness & awareness, usually interested in all aspects of the mystical psychic forces, has the potential to apply spirituality in a grounded way, willing to serve others in a healing way, healers & psychics are found in this group.

White: Godly
Also - spiritually elevated, motivated, cleanliness, purity & innocence, detachment, reflects all colors.
Pink: These people are quiet, refined, modest and fond of beauty, gifted of great devotion and much self-sacrifice.

Yellow: Thinking, Smart & Intelligent
Also - supersensitive people, highly nervous, optimistic, and very capable in business. They could be too generous. They also have a sense of reason, logic & assessment, grasp things easily, controlling & dominating.

Aura Overview

<u>Auric Body</u>
Etheric
- Anatomy
- Whitish, Light silvery blue

Emotional
- Feelings
- Many colors and can change with a person's mood

Mental
- Thoughts
- Yellow

Astral
- Doorway to our spiritual side
- Silver thread

Etheric Template
- Blueprint of our physical, emotional & mental
- Light cobalt blue

Celestial
- Pure love
- Shimmery, beautiful light

Ketheric Template
- Blueprint of our life purpose & lessons
- Golden

The Most Famous Proof of Auras

The halo of Mother Mary and her son, Jesus

Chakras

In Ayurveda Medicine each of the seven auric layers corresponds to a Chakra.

Once all outside information comes through the Vital Field (Aura) then it is channeled via the Chakra System!

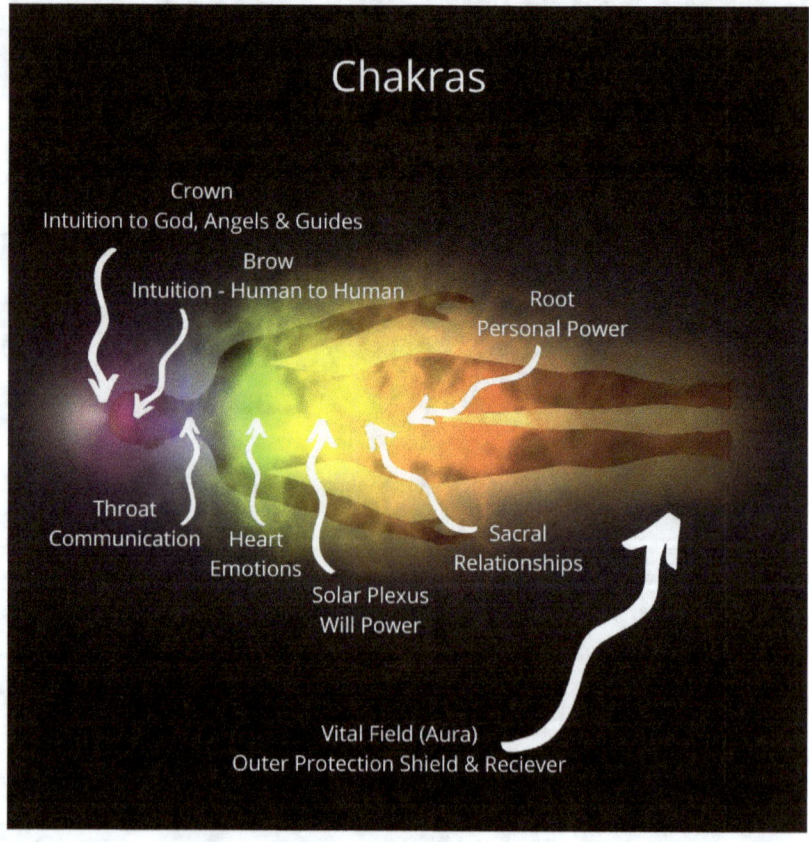

(For more information on Chakras, read my Secrets of a Healer – Magic of Reiki Book)

Meridians

Once the information is channeled through the appropriate Chakra, it travels through a corresponding meridian channel, which in turn takes the energy to the appropriate organ for healing **OR** endocrine gland for communication.

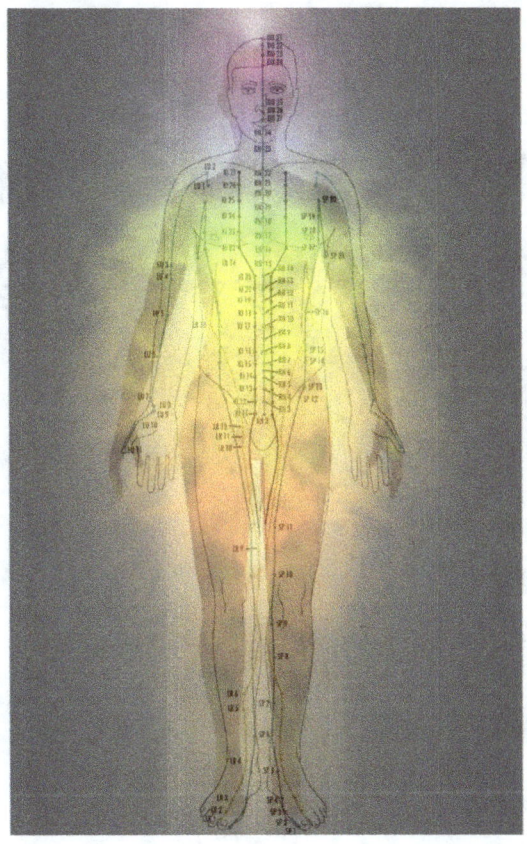

(For more information on Meridians, read my Secrets of a Healer – Magic of Muscle Testing Book)

Astral-Etheric Vibration

Prayer
Is talking
Meditation
Is listening

Raising Your Vibratory Rate

Raising your vibratory rate can be done on four different levels.
- ✓ **Physical** – with food, exercise, breath, massage, body aligning, aromatherapy, color, crystals, energy healing (Reiki), music (sound therapy), and vitamins, to name a few
- ✓ **Mental** – with positive thinking, knowledge
- ✓ **Emotional** – with releasing any negative emotional blocks
- ✓ **Spiritual** – with prayer, meditation

A person needs to be ready and willing, but the most important thing is that they need to be balanced (emotionally, mentally, physically, and spiritually).

All modalities will change a person's vibratory rate, which in turn will balance (sympathetic or parasympathetic) the body so it can be enlightened.

Breath

Breath is life-force energy, the basis for life. We can live many days without food, a few days without water and only moments without air.

The way you breathe will tell a person many things about you. You may be a shallow breather, which shows impatience. A deep, heavy breather shows intent. Your breathing also determines how well you manifest, create, or interpret energy.

Your breath is one of the main catalysts for changing your vibration. Before I ask an intuitive question or have an intent, I take a deep breath.

Natural Breathing

Babies breathe in this complete, natural manner. Adults, with their penchant for tight clothing, a sedentary, stressful lifestyle, and poor posture, have tended to move away from this form of breathing.

The following Yoga exercise, with practice, will become almost automatic.

Thought Energy

NEGATIVE/POSITIVE ENERGY

What about negative energy? Negative energy seems to have the easiest access to you when you are not in control. Examples of not being in control include being under the influence of any alcohol, illegal drugs, some medication, orgasm (uncommitted – without love), unguided trance or meditation and the dream state. Why do you think prayers to be said before going to bed were created? It only takes a moment to protect yourself. Say a quick affirmation/prayer/statement before bed, traveling or at any other time you think you may need it. This does not assist other people unless they are directly involved with you.

I was traveling up north to teach a course and when I was seated on the plane, I cleared any negative energy on the entire plane. But when I was coming home, I was only allowed to clear the walkway that led to my seat and from the seat beside me. (A spirit guide told me that I could not clear the whole plane). In the first plane, perhaps the airplane itself was a problem which would have affected not only me, but also the other passengers; however, in the second plane there was not going to be anything other than the seat beside me and the walkway to the exit door that would have created problems for me.

I do pray/ask for my food to be blessed before I eat it. I was at a fellow classmate's one night for dinner, she served a delicious meal. I was telling her and her husband how, with a pendulum (a small weighted object that is tied to a chain or string), to count the vibration of anything. They had asked if I would show them how this could be done. I started with holding the pendulum over my salad and asked the pendulum to swing to the number at which the salad was vibrating. (I start the pendulum to swing in a straight line - back and forth counts as one. I count 1, 2, 3, 4... to 10, by tens to 100, then by hundreds and so forth until the pendulum swings clockwise for positive vibration or counterclockwise for negative vibration.)

I was counting the salad's vibration from one up, and I was on one hundred, when suddenly; the pendulum picked up speed and was swinging so fast that it caught me off guard. I looked up at them with an astonished look and when my friend started to laugh, I told her I did not understand what had just happened and she explained, "I just blessed the salad." Well, from that moment on, I understood why I was to pray before eating!

Intent

Positive thoughts or intent will create positive outcomes and your vibration will be higher. Negative thoughts or intent create negative outcomes and your vibration will be lower.

Intent is 100% of the game.

Section Two
Learning To Listen

GETTING ANSWERS

Once you have raised your vibration, there are many ways a person can find the answers for which he or she is searching for. This section focuses on how to receive answers for yourself or others.

FIRST RULE is that you must ask a LITERAL QUESTION. The mind and creator/spirit is extremely literal. If you ask, "Can I <u>help</u> this client?" or, "Can I <u>cure</u> this client?", you will find that these are two very different questions. The words you use in your question will be interpreted literally. Our everyday language contains a lot of slang which is intended to have the same meaning as formal English but frequently this is not the case.

SECOND RULE the TIME FRAME is particularly important. If you ask, "Can I cure this client?" and the answer is "yes", did you ask "Today?" Try to be specific and to the point. This may take a lot of practice.
THIRD RULE write down your questions, so when you receive an answer you can re-check if you were specific enough.

Following are many ways to practice the technique of seeing, hearing, feeling, or knowing an answer to your question.

Exercise #1 – *Visual* – Complimentary Colors

To show you what a Complimentary Color looks like.

Procedure:
1. Get colored paper
2. Put it against a white background
3. Stare at the paper for the count of thirty (30 seconds or longer)
4. Look away from the colored paper, and in a moment, you will see the complimentary color

    Some of these pairings are:
    - ✓ Blue you will see Orange.
    - ✓ Red is Green,
    - ✓ Yellow is Purple,
    - ✓ White is Black, etc.

Of course, different shades will give different shades of the complimentary (opposite) color.

The Color you see is <u>NOT</u> an Aura!
Again, these are the complimentary colors you are seeing.

*If someone is wearing a yellow shirt and you see purple around them, you are likely seeing the complimentary color, not the Aura. BUT, if you see blue or any other color than purple, then you are seeing the Aura.

Exercise #2 – *Visual* – Aura

Seeing an Aura.

Procedure:
1. Have someone stand against a white wall. Semi dark, minimal light seems to be the easiest to see the aura.
2. Stand approximately 10-15 feet away from them. It is best if you can be in front of them instead of at an angle.
3. Focus your eyes about a hand above their head and then just stare.
4. Look with artist eyes (relaxed, dis-focused, like you are going to look at a 3D picture).

You are most likely looking at the persons Etheric Body, this is the simplest part of the aura to see. Try not to move your eyes around, yes...blinking is okay.

Notice the white glow around them...it is usually about 1/4" to 3" inches around them or to one side (can be bigger or smaller in different areas around the body). It may move up, down, to one side or the other while you are looking.

Try not to change the focus of your eyes, stay gazing about a hand above their head.

Do not fret if you cannot see it, just keep practicing by trying different people.

Exercise #3 – *Visual* – Intuitive Art

Intuitive Art Development using color.
You will need: A music player with 3 different types of music, 5 pieces of colored paper (construction paper works well, and it does not matter what color; all the same or all different) and many different colored chalks, felts, or crayons, etc.

Procedure:
1. Choose 1 piece of colored paper. Place on table in front of you.
2. Choose 3 coloring tools (3 chalks, etc. if using chalk place on tissue).
3. Know exactly where your paper and coloring tools are.
4. Turn on the first music choice.
5. CLOSE YOUR EYES and draw whatever comes from listening to the music. Timing approx. 3 minutes.
6. Stop, put paper away for now.
7. Repeat steps 1-5 with second choice of music on a second piece of paper.
8. Repeat steps 1-5 with third choice of music on a third piece of paper. This time KEEP EYES OPEN.
9. Repeat steps 1-5, but this time with no music, just think of a person.
10. Repeat step 9, but this time with a person sitting in front of you (do their energy).

11. Stop; release your energy of coloring (take a deep breath with the intent of letting go).
12. You may now go back and look at what you have drawn. What you drew in color, is energy from music and of a person. If you want to analyze what you have drawn go to the colors of an aura. The paper color choice also counts.

✓ Aura drawings
   a. Are usually done on onion paper or similar.
   b. The coloring tool used is usually chalk.
   c. When coloring with different colored chalks and not to have the chalks blend to make black, use a spray sealant to hold the color you want, and let it dry a few seconds,
   d. Then continue coloring,
   e. Use sealant when finished.

Aura drawings are not usually specific, usually very abstract.

Exercise #4 – *Visual* – Practice Your Intuition

This is something you can try, to improve your intuitive abilities.

Here is what you are going to need:
- ✓ White cardboard – (same thickness as a file folder,) white is best.
- ✓ Black pen

1. Cut the cardboard into 10 card size pieces.
2. Draw a (one on each of the five cards):
    a. Square
    b. Star
    c. Waves
    d. Triangle
    e. Circle

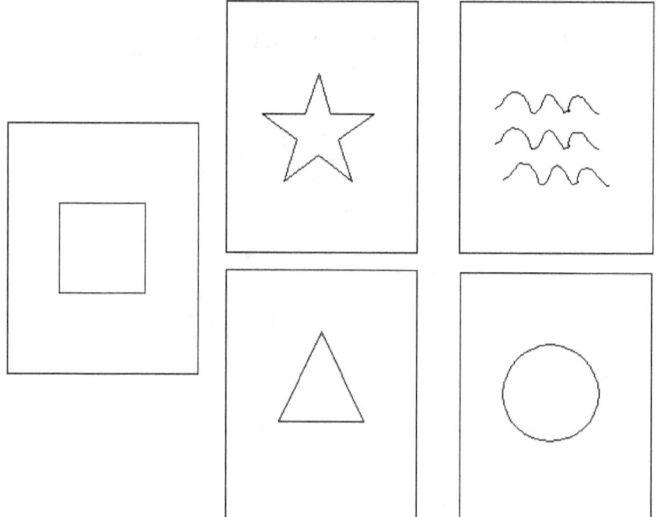

3. Take <u>one</u> of the five drawn on cards, and stare at it for 60 seconds.
4. Now, turn all the cards over so the tops are blank.
5. Mix the cards up.
6. Move the cards apart so that all ten cards are not touching each other or overlapping.
7. Take a moment and stare at each card.
8. Pick your card.

What can happen is the drawing will appear as if it jumped out through the back of the card. For some people, it is as if you can see through the cards, though there are many people who cannot see anything at all.

Practice, practice, practice!

Exercise #5 – *Feeler* – Breath A

1. Begin by sitting or standing straight (in a good posture).
2. Take a breath through your nose.
    As you inhale,
    a. First fill the lower section of your lungs. Your diaphragm will push your abdomen out to make room for the air.
    b. Second, fill the middle part of your lungs as your lower ribs and chest move forward slightly to accommodate the air.
    c. Third, fill the upper part of your lungs as you raise your chest slightly and draw in your abdomen a little to support your lungs.
    These three steps can be performed in one smooth, continuous inhalation which, with practice, can be completed in a couple of seconds.
3. Hold your breath for a few seconds.
4. As you exhale slowly, pull your abdomen in slightly and lift it up slowly as the lungs empty.
5. When you have completely exhaled, relax your abdomen and chest.
6. At the end of the inhalation phase, raise your shoulders and collarbone slightly so that you are sure that the very top of your lungs are replenished with fresh air.

EVERY TIME YOU TAKE THREE DEEP BREATHS, YOU RAISE YOUR VIBRATORY RATE!

AND WITHOUT TAKING THE THREE BREATHS YOU WILL NOT SHIFT YOUR VIBRATION.

Exercise #6 – *Feeler* – Breath B

This is not a yoga breath; this technique is for a different purpose.

1. Get a feather, an ostrich feather, a nice fluffy one works best.
2. Imagine or hold the feather out in front of you about 12 inches or 30 cm.
3. Take a breath (actually, this time take a breath no matter if you have the feather or just imagining one).

Notice how you breathe when you inhale and when you exhale.

Notice if your mouth is open or closed when you took that breath. Did the feather move?

This exercise will show you how much energy you put forth when you take a breath or if you are holding in your emotions.

> PURPOSE - You NEED to open your mouth when you are letting go of negative emotions. This action will allow the negative energy to escape with your breath and release the negative energy from the cells of your body. (*Think about what happens when you hold your breath. Not much happens; a person does not release enough energy to change the situation*).
>
> PURPOSE - To manifest or create, your breath will need to move that feather. According to your

intent, when you take a breath, it is a signal for change. No matter if it is to change a conversation, to run, to swim, to speak publicly, to sing, to say, "I love you", or to make a deal...? The cosmic signal for change is a deep breath with air movement.

Exercise #7 – *Feeler* – Pendulum

A pendulum is defined as a weight hung from a fixed point so that it can swing freely, and specifically refers to a rod with a weight at the end that regulates the mechanism of a clock.

If we use a similar idea to the clock and the pendulum is tuned to your personal vibration by allowing the string to slip loosely through the *thumb, middle, and pointer fingers* until it appears to swing. Instead of a rod, we will be using a weight on a string. The pendulum's string should be no longer than the distance of you holding the string in your fingers and your elbow resting on a table; the pendulum should not hit the table.

You can buy a pendulum or make your own. A necklace will work also.

To make a pendulum you will need:
- ✓ Thread (gold or silver color elastic heavy thread works very well) or chain
- ✓ Hot glue and gun or solder gun
- ✓ Beads (one large oblong bead, metal cover, three to five smaller beads)

Making A Pendulum Procedure:
1. Cut the thread to approximately 10 inches.
2. Attach one end of the thread to the larger bead.

3. Place metal or plastic cover over the larger bead and through the thread.
4. Glue together.
5. Arrange the remaining beads on the thread.
6. Place your elbow on a table.
7. Hold the thread so that the beads dangle.
8. The large bead should swing easily without touching the table.
9. Fold the thread at your fingertips.
10. Loop the folded end around and through to create a knot.
11. Pull tight.
12. Cut off the remaining loose thread approximately ¼ inch from the knot.

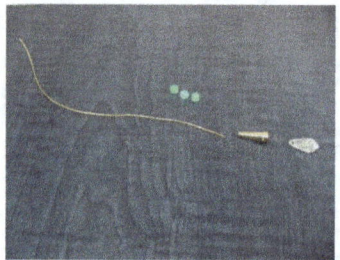 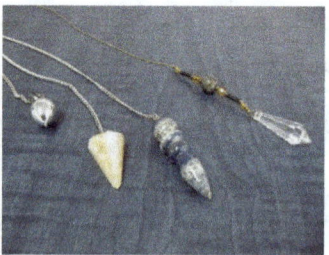

Your brain is like a highly developed computer, unconsciously knowing everything it has ever seen, heard, felt, or thought since conception to now and, if you believe in past lives, that also. So, when we program our bodies to answer in a 'yes' or 'no' function, it will do just that. Every person has the answers to his/her own situation; he/she just needs to be shown how to ask the right questions.

PROCEDURE
To check the rotation of your pendulum:

You can program the pendulum any way you like as long as the direction is ALWAYS the same for the 'yes' or 'no' answer. E.g. Circle for 'yes', straight line for 'no'.

OR, here is another exercise to try (from Hannah Kroeger).
1. Draw one of your hands on a piece of paper and mark + and - as drawn in this picture.

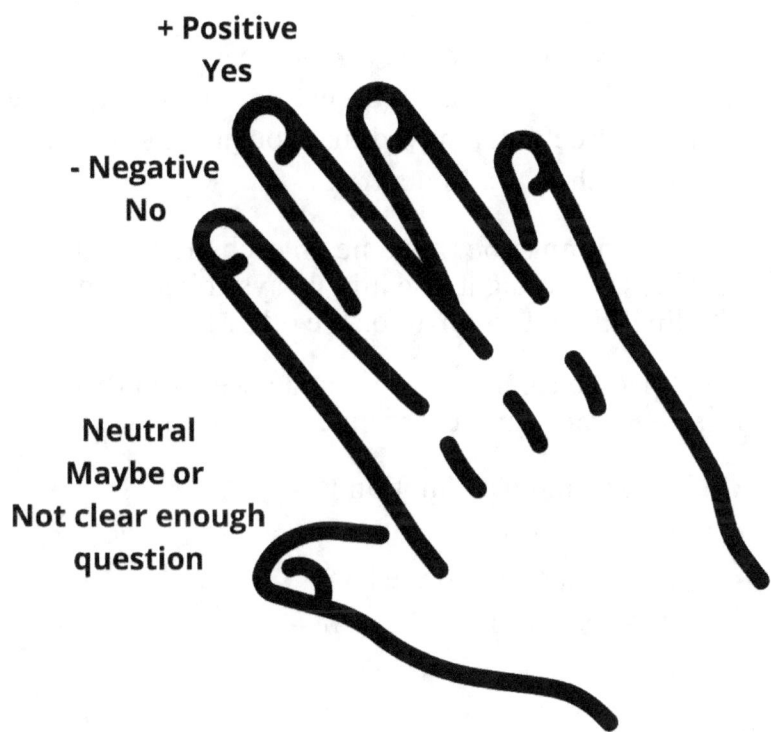

2. Place your hand on the paper and hold the pendulum above + positive (yes)
    - Say out loud show me a yes
    - Watch which direction it moves in (make note of the direction)
2. With your hand on the paper and holding the pendulum above the + negative(no)
    - Say show me a no
    - Watch which direction it moves in (make note of the direction)
3. With your hand on paper and this time holding the pendulum above + neutral (Means – maybe, do not know, or that you need to ask a better question)
    - Say show me a neutral
    - Watch how it moves
4. Now do it again on all three; test that you have the same directional moved that you had the first time with each, =, -, and neutral.

The movement must be the same on each individual finger. If yes is a straight line it is always going to be a straight line!!!! And so forth for the other fingers.

Different people can have different answers (all that matters is the movement for you).

- forward and back motion
- sideways motion
- rotate in a circle to the left
- rotate in a circle to the right
- stop dead

It does not matter what other people's pendulum swing is doing, just yours!

You can ask the pendulum to show you a bigger movement.

You can stop the pendulum and ask for the next finger or just go to the next finger.

    5. Now take your hand away and ask the pendulum to show you each (yes, no, and neutral) one at a time without the paper.

Practice until you know what each is, and movement is that same way every single time.

    6. Now test the pendulum with questions.

    Is my (your name) _____? Wait for the answer.

If it answered correctly try another.

    Am I (you) wearing socks today? Wait for the answer.

I <u>always</u> test a pendulum 3x before I ask an important question. And I also say honest and with integrity.

    Is my name _____?

    Am I on today? (Meaning can I answer these questions)

    Any questions that I really know the answer to?

A couple of other things you can try using a pendulum...

The vibration of an object compared to your body

1. This first action is to program your brain. Literally and on purpose, move the pendulum in a back and forward motion. Practice.
    a. The count is a <u>full</u> back and forward motion for 1
    b. So, every time it comes forward you count 1, 2, 3 (only on the forward movement).
    c. The objective is to find the number that corresponds to the vibration of the object. Now say, show me if it is a + or – (manually move the pendulum on purpose clockwise for positive vibration and counter for negative vibration).
2. Now, hold the pendulum over something
    a. eg. A pen
3. Start to count
   I count 1-20 and then by tens, hundreds, and so forth... (to speed up my counting)
   1 2 3 4 5 6 7 8 9 10
   11 12 13 1 4 15 16 17 18 19 20
   30 40 50 60 70 80 90 100
   200, 300 400....
   1000 2000 3000...
   10,000 20,000...
   100,000 200,000...
   1, 000,000 2,000,000...
4. When the pendulum has reached the appropriate number, it will turn either of the two directions in a circular motion.
    a. clockwise for positive vibration and counter for negative vibration

What this means is the item will lower your vibration, especially if you eat it. As an example, you are using the pendulum to find the vibration of a banana, and the peel is on the banana. The pendulum would swing to the negative, as the peel is poisonous to you if you ate it. And without the peel on the banana, the pendulum will swing to the positive.

Scale

This is used to answer a question for days, weeks, months, amounts, etc. You can draw any number of lines on the scale that you need.

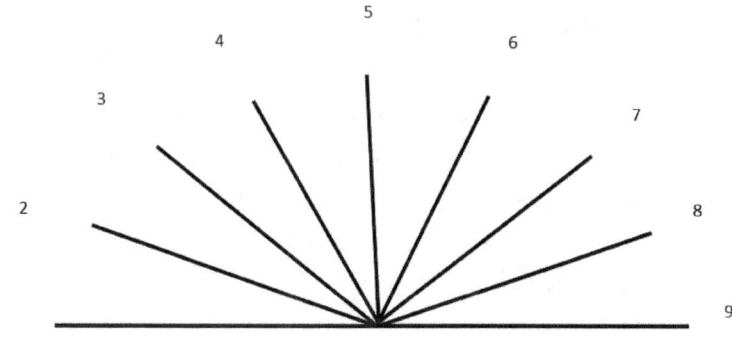

1. Hold the pendulum in the center on the bottom straight line 1____9
2. Ask the question
3. Wait to see the direction of the answer.

Exercise #8 – *Feeler* – Body Pendulum

This tool can **only** be used with a 'yes' or 'no' answer.

Make sure you are very specific (After a dream I had I asked if I should move the school and it said 'no' but then I asked should I move all the contents in the school and it said 'yes'.) The answers are always extremely literal. *The building/school (bricks and wood) should not move.* When asking a personal question, make sure to ask for an honest and unbiased answer.

It does not always work on yourself. Your conscious mind knows what answer it wants. You can also do this with your client just thinking the question and you answering. This is a great tool for finding out a person's channel of communication.

Procedure:
1. **To start:** Physically have your body lean forward from the ankles (like you are as stiff as a piece of two-by-four wood) saying, "Forward without falling is a 'yes'," and then lean your body backward saying, "backward without falling is a 'no'." Do this three times.
2. Vitamins are great to use while learning this because the vibratory rate is so high.

3. Now, ask this question while holding the vitamins to your stomach, "Is this vitamin(s) what my body needs to have today?" Make sure your knees are relaxed and are locked neither too tightly nor loosely, just comfortably.
4. Now allow your body to move, it will either go forward or backward for the 'yes' or 'no' answer. If your body goes side to side, it means you need to ask a more specific or a better question.

Try this with 5 – 10 different kinds of vitamins. When you feel confident and you can tell the difference between 'yes' and 'no', try candy or your name (if you answer incorrectly to your name, make sure you say, "in this life time"), or ask any other **very specific** single answer question you want answered.

(From my book – Secrets of a Healer – Magic of Muscle Testing)

Exercise #9 – *Audio* – Automatic Writing

This technique is used to gain more information than just a 'yes' or 'no' answer. Some people use this technique to release useless information gained over the day/week/years, to journal their thoughts or to receive insight.

Procedure:
1. Write out a detailed question to which you would like an answer.
2. Take three deep breaths.
3. Relax your body.
4. Send your intent /thought up through your crown chakra.
5. Ask your angels/guides/God, or whomever you would like, to help you with the answer.
6. Bring the intent/thought back down through your crown chakra down through your hand that holds your pen.
7. Now write whatever comes to mind or whatever your hand wants to write (let go of your control).

Practice...Practice... Practice... (If you try to control this, it doesn't work, so don't worry about spelling or correct English).

This technique can also be used for channeling.
 * Take care in realizing who is answering you...is it a high spirit or a low spirit?

These next exercises will help you notice energy (from my Secrets of a Healer – Magic of Reiki Book)

Exercise #10 – *Knower–* Thought Energy A

1. Walk around the room like you NORMALLY would.
   - Notice how you feel.
2. Stop and take a breath.
3. Now, have your intent or thought change to walking as if your feet have cords that are growing out of them like TREE ROOTS that tie to the center of the Earth. Now walk around the room and notice if you sense any difference.
   - Again, notice how you feel.
4. Stop and take a breath.
5. Now, have your intent change to walking as if you are as light as a FEATHER, no weight at all. Again, walk around the room and notice if you sense any difference.
   - Notice how you feel.
6. Once you have tried all three, take a breath and let go of the experience and go back to your original way of how you want to be now.

Exercise #11 – *Knower* – Thought Energy B

1. With a partner,
    a. Stand facing each other.
    b. Have your partner stand normal.
    c. Lightly with one hand move them at their shoulder. Push them backward (be careful not to push them over... LIGHTLY).
2. Now, have them think or imagine that their feet have cords that grow out of them like tree roots that tie to the center of the Earth. Now, lightly with your hand move them at their shoulder. Push them backward again.
    - Notice any difference?
3. Now, have them think that they are as light as a feather, then lightly with your hand move them at their shoulder. Push them backward again.
    - Notice any difference?
4. Have them take a breath and go back to normal.

If you do not notice any difference, try a few more people. The purpose of these exercises is to show you what you think can change your energy field. Yes, even gravitational.

Interesting! What we think, is what we create. As I say, "Be careful what you think, you might just get it".

Exercise #12 – *Knower* – Psychometry

The definition of psychometry is divination from personal, physical contact with an object, of the charter of the object, or people connected with it.

This term refers to bursts of energy and or memories, both negative and positive, which have left an "imprint" upon an object or place. For instance, a house where a traumatic experience has happened, such as a murder or suicide, may feel distinctly chilled or "bad", while a favorite childhood toy or play area may feel light or "good". A place or thing may be so charged with emotions and memories that it may even seem haunted. It might also be considered a form of precognition in reverse accomplished by touching a specific object.

"Mind measure" is the ability to sense and interpret mental vibrations recorded in a physical object, or in a certain place. It may be noted that all the sensing faculties of the astral – mental level register communication from the mind to mind. They may not be reliable, since the mind at this level can be conditioned by false thinking.

Procedure:
Hold the object (piece of paper, jewelry or picture) in your hands for a few moments and then begin to write down any visions, thoughts, or feelings that you are receiving from the object you are holding. Trust your first

impressions and record them, no matter how little you are getting. Sometimes just starting to write or say what you are receiving will start the flow of the message(s).

WRITTEN NAME

Procedure:
1. Cut three or four pieces of paper to the same size (approximately 2"x 3" rectangle).
2. Have four different people sign their name on a piece of paper (have one signature on each piece of paper).
3. Once you have all the papers signed, fold the papers the same way.
4. Mix up the papers.
5. Choose one.
6. Hold on to the paper and write down the answers to these questions: (in your mind ask the questions and wait for the answer)
   - ✓ Color of the person's hair, dark or light?
   - ✓ Color of the eyes, dark or medium or blue?
   - ✓ How tall is the person?
   - ✓ What is the person's occupation?
   - ✓ Does he/she have children?
   - ✓ Is the person married?
   - ✓ And anything else you can think of to ask.

Continue to interpret all the pieces of paper in the same manner.

JEWELRY

Procedure:
1. Have three friends bring you a piece of jewelry that you have not seen before. These people must have personal information about the person who owns the jewelry.
2. Hold on to one item and wait a moment for any sense to come.
3. Then write it down. You can ask the same type of questions as in number 1.
4. Repeat on other pieces of jewelry.

My husband was in a class, years ago, that was practicing this technique and came home saying that it was a terrible experience, that the person trying to read his wedding ring had nothing correct about him at all. A few minutes later I started to laugh. He looked at me as if I was crazy. With a more serious face, I reminded him we just bought the ring a couple of months earlier in Vegas...at a pawn shop. (Nick had had his original ring stolen at a volleyball game years before and we had never replaced it.) The point is that this ring had no connection to Nick. The vibrations were those of the original owner.

PHOTOGRAPH

Procedure:
1. Have photographs of three different persons whom you do not know; the photographs should allow you to look into the eyes.
2. Hold the first photograph and notice the first thing or emotion you sense.
3. Write it down.
4. Look into the eyes and ask the same type of questions as in the other two exercises.
5. Repeat with the other photographs.

When you have finished your recording, check off how many questions you answered correctly. You are aiming for perfection. Being correct less than 90% of the time is just not good enough. Personally, I do not believe I "have" the person unless I am at least 98-99% correct.

**Practice...Practice...Practice.
This technique takes a great deal of practice.**

Astral Projection

Just before falling asleep at night seems to be when most people have these occurrences. In astral projection, the astral body leaves the physical body. The dream state is believed to be in the astral level. The astral body is one of seven sheath bodies or auric layers (shown in the aura picture). We all have physical, mental, astral, etheric, emotional, spiritual, and casual bodies. In astral projection, many believe you remain attached by a silver "umbilical type" cord to your physical body. *When I travel, I personally do not take notice of any cord. No matter what...I have always come back.*

I wanted to have proof that I astral traveled.
The first-time testing if I really did travel, I had a friend of mine hypnotize me and told me to stand by him and see myself. Well, I tried and tried to see myself...it was a little hard with my eyes closed. When I came out of the hypnotic state and thought about what happened, I knew we were on the wrong track because I was trying to see out of my closed eyes in real life.

A few weeks later we tried again. This time, my friend, his wife, Nick (my husband) and I were in my living room when he hypnotized me a second time. I didn't try to see myself this time. He asked me to astral travel and stand across the room. As I imagined myself standing across the room from where I was sitting, my dog barked. Quite quickly my attention popped back into my own body. My friend brought me fully out of the hypnosis and had me open my eyes.

They all were sitting on the edge of their seats staring at me. He asked me where I imagined I was standing. I told him across the room and pointed directly to the spot. They looked at each other with astonishment...excitedly I asked why, what had happened. They went on to explain to me that the dog started barking at the wall and our cat, was sitting on the love seat beside my friend's wife, jumped up in a Halloween cat pose, hissing at the same spot as the barking dog!

Great! I had done it and with proof from my own animals. The only question now to be answered was why my animals had not recognized me. Interesting!

I had had other experiences before this, but I had no proof of what astral traveling was.

Exercise #13 – *Knower & Visual* – Remote Viewing

Remote Viewing is used by you Astral traveling. I have used this technique with a location.

I was going to teach in Dawson City, Yukon and I thought it would be a great opportunity to see if I could astral travel/remote view where I was going to be staying and teaching since I had never been there and had not seen pictures.

I made myself comfortable and relaxed my body. Then I stated the location of the hotel, took a deep breath and saw in my mind (like I was dreaming) a door and as I went in, I saw a second door. To my right was the reception desk, behind that was food on a table like in a restaurant, to my left was the conference room and stairs.

When I arrived, to my delight, there were the two doors (they were needed to keep the cold out in winter) and I had imagined the reception desk correctly. Behind the wall of the reception desk was a bar that served food... correct again! (The real restaurant was to the left and a short distance down the hall.) The conference room was to the left, although we did not use that location due to a small class size; instead, we ascended the stairs and turned into the first room on the left.

I had not seen it as clearly as it really happened, but I was correct on all accounts, just as I was seeing it in code.

Procedure:

1. Pick a location that you want to scan. One that you can go and check out and see how accurate you were.

2. Make yourself comfortable...
3. Relax...
4. Concentrate on your breathing. As it goes <u>in... and out...</u> (*Say this underlined part three times slowly.*)
5. Notice your feet...breathe all the way down to your feet...slowly...
6. Relax...let go...
7. With your next breath, imagine that you are the size of a pea, in the middle of your head.
8. Imagine that you astral traveled out of your crown chakra (top of your head) and teleport to wherever you intended to be going.
9. Write down the first thing you sense (see, feel, hear, know, smell, or taste) or say it to someone writing for you.
10. Turn around in all directions and write down the first thing you sense.
11. Once you are finished, take a deep breath, and wiggle your toes, coming perfectly back into your body.
12. Open your eyes.

Exercise #14 – *Knower & Feeler* – Body Scan

This is also called Medical Intuitive or Psi Scanis and is used to scan a person's body to discover any dis-ease, past or present.

Procedure:

Have the reader write down a name (first and last), age and city of a person you do not know. *** You need someone to read this to you. (Reader, do not read out loud the words that are *italicized*.)

1. Make yourself comfortable...
2. Relax...
3. Concentrate on your breathing. As it goes <u>in... and out</u>... (*Say this underlined part three times slowly.*)
4. Notice your feet...breathe all the way down to your feet...slowly...
5. Relax...let go...
6. If you have any personal thoughts that creep into your mind while you are relaxing...tell them you'll look at them later...
7. Tell me when you are relaxed and ready to scan...just say, "I'm ready" ... (*When they say ready, read the next section.*)
8. I would like you to sense, feel, see, know, or hear the body of.... (*Give name, age, and city of the person being scanned.*)
9. If all you have is a picture, or sense in your head, that will work... also just the intent will do.

10. (*Give the Scanner time to sense the body and then ask:*) As you sense this body, to what areas of the body is your attention immediately attracted? (*Make notes of he/she is saying to you on your paper.*) Follow up with I would like you to focus your attention now on the:

- ✓ **Skeletal System** — do any bone or structure problems exist…you might see a color…feel your own body reacting…just know what is wrong…or a voice in your head tells you… (*Make sure to write down whatever you are told.*)
- ✓ **Muscular System** — muscles… (*If he or she does not say anything, just continue.*)
- ✓ **Nervous System** — brain, hypothalamus, spinal cord, nerves…
- ✓ **Circulatory System** — heart, arteries, veins…
- ✓ **Urinary System** — kidneys, bladder, ureter, urethra…
- ✓ **Reproductive System** —
- ✓ **for a *woman*** - uterus, ovaries, fallopian tubes, vagina…
- ✓ **for a *man*** - prostrate, testicles, scrotum, seminal vesicles…
- ✓ **Digestive System** — salivary glands, pharynx, esophagus, liver, gall bladder, duodenum, stomach, small intestine, pancreas, appendix, ascending colon, transverse colon, descending colon, or rectum…
- ✓ **Endocrine System** — pituitary gland, pineal, thyroid, parathyroid, thymus, adrenal, pancreas, ovaries, testes…

- ✓ **Immune and Lymphatic System** — tonsils, sub-maxillary lymph nodes, axially lymph nodes, spleen, lymph vessels, lymph nodes, left thoracic duct, right thoracic duct, inguinal lymph nodes...
- ✓ **Respiratory System** — nose, trachea, bronchi, bronchioles, lung, diaphragm...
- ✓ **Sensory System** — eyes, ears, smell, touch, taste...

11. Now change your focus, and describe the mental, emotional, and spiritual nature of the person being scanned...you may go into as much detail as you like...
12. *When no more information is forthcoming:*
13. Fill this person's body with healing white light for his/her highest good...
14. When you have done that, fill and surround yourself with the healing white light...
15. We are finished...take one deep breath...wiggle your toes...and open your eyes...
16. When you open your eyes, you will feel great...better than ever before...
    - o ***You can do this also with a place (use Earth grids, as on a map) or items.

Exercise #15
– *Knower, Visual, Audio & Feeler* – Animal Sensing

Procedure:

1. You are going to imagine an animal, any animal of your choice.
2. Make yourself comfortable...
3. Relax...
4. Concentrate on your breathing. As it goes <u>in...</u> <u>and out...</u> (*Say this underlined part three times slowly.*)
5. Notice your feet...breathe all the way down to your feet...slowly...
6. Relax...let go...
7. With your next breath, imagine that you are the size of a pea, in the middle of your head.
8. Imagine that you astral traveled out of your crown chakra (top of your head) and teleport to wherever in the world your animal is.
9. You enter the animal through their crown chakra, making sure you are looking out their eyes.
10. Write down the first thing you sense (see, feel, hear, know, smell, or taste) or say it to someone writing for you.
11. Turn around in all directions and write down the first thing you sense.
12. Imagine what the animal does all day. You can fast forward, rewind, or stop at any time by just thinking it.
13. Once you are finished, take a deep breath, and wiggle your toes, coming out of them and going

perfectly back into your body.
14. Open your eyes and thank the animal for the experience.

Journal your experience and try different animals. You may be able to gain insight on what makes that specific animal breed good at (jumping, running, hunting, etc.). These traits may be helpful to you in your life, run faster, etc.

Exercise #16
– *Audio, Feeler, Knower & Visual* –
Psychic Detective

Can be a great tool if you are doing investigative work for the police.

Procedure:

1. You are going to imagine the person (ask your angels for protection).
2. Make yourself comfortable...
3. Relax...
4. Concentrate on your breathing. As it goes <u>in... and out</u>... (*Say this underlined part three times slowly.*)
5. Notice your feet...breathe all the way down to your feet...slowly...
6. Relax...let go...
7. With your next breath, imagine that you are the size of a pea, in the middle of your head.
8. Imagine that you astral traveled out of your crown chakra (top of your head) and teleport to wherever in the world the person is.
9. You enter the other person through their crown chakra, making sure you are looking out of their eyes.
10. Write down the first thing you sense (see, feel, hear, know, smell, or taste) or say it to someone writing for you.
11. Turn around in all directions and write down the first thing you sense.
12. Imagine what they do all day. You can fast

forward, rewind, or stop at any time by just thinking it. You can rewind to the time of the crime or murder, what did you sense.
13. Once you are finished, take a deep breath, and wiggle your toes, coming out of them and going perfectly back into your body.
14. Open your eyes and thank the angels for their help in the experience.

ONLY do this if you are serious about giving the information to the police. Spirit only helps those that are sincere.

When I first started, I tried this three times. By the third time I knew I didn't like the feeling of knowing this information and how the family felt, and never continued in this line of work.

Section Three Prophecy Psychic Readings

– Audio, Feeler, Knower & Visual –

Most people go to a psychic reader to receive confirmation, direction, and guidance. They are at a point in their life where they need spiritual help. Help from a higher power in changing their Physical, Mental, Emotional, and Spiritual state. Even though their Ketheric Template cannot be changed you can help them understand how to change their Etheric Template!

The person (*Astral Body*) can connect to their (*Etheric, Emotional, and Mental Body*), but many people do not know how to connect with both their (*Template*s) because their (*Celestial Body*) gets in the way.

This is where you will come in, you are the missing piece, to them building their dream home. You are the facilitator to connect and change their lower self with their higher self, until they learn how to do it themselves.

The biggest secret to E.S.P. or intuitive energy is to just allow the information to come uncensored and unbiased (like a B.S. story). Because if you stop and think about what you are receiving, two things will happen. First, you are now using your conscious mind instead of the subconscious mind.

Your conscious mind is the part of your brain over which you have control, moving, eating, watching T.V. and going for a drive, are all examples of your conscious mind at work. Your subconscious mind is what the brain uses without your control – like your heart beating, breathing and digestion. Another example is when you drive the same route day after day, and suddenly you notice your surroundings, you were daydreaming. Your subconscious mind was driving instead of your conscious mind. Even your morals are part of your subconscious mind, as that is where your deepest beliefs are embedded. Not even a hypnotist can make you do something that you morally would not do or that could harm you (this is because your deep-rooted morals are in your subconscious mind).

And the second thing that happens is that when you break the connection or change the spiritual information, spirits stop communicating with you.

Because I wanted to know for sure that what I had learned was real and not just a fictional story, I decided it was time to practice on people.

I had to decide on whom to practice... family and friends? I was concerned it would become confusing determining if what I was getting was from their energy or because it was something in my memory, I already knew lots about them. I also cared about what would come out of my mouth. I did not want to offend them or hurt their feelings and I still wanted to maintain our close relationships.

So, my decision was to put an ad in the classified section of the newspaper offering psychic readings by donation. I had nothing to lose, and that way I could practice on a stranger about whom I knew nothing about and see if this intuitive ability was real. If a person did not like it or thought I was a fake, there would be no charge.

To my astonishment, reading strangers was thrilling and I was perfectly accurate with almost all my clients. After having read for about two hundred clients, I decided that E.S.P. was real and that every psychic should have a counselling degree.

My integrity always made me strive for the truth, and only the truth. Anyone can make up compelling stories about past lives or future, for there is not any proof. You can even have a pretty accurate guess of the present just by reading the person's body language, clothing, and speech of the person sitting in front of you.

There is one thing that a psychic cannot make up — childhood memories. No two people have had the same life experiences at similar ages, even twins.

I would always give as much information as I could about what I was seeing, feeling, hearing, and knowing. The scenery, if there were other people or animals around, smells, sounds, descriptions of clothing, length and color of hair, emotions, walking pattern, anything that would prove that I had their past.

I usually tape recorded my readings for the client so he or she could refer to them later.

A few times a client would say that my description did not match his or her memories. I would give three to four examples of different childhood ages and if he or she could not remember or not be able to confirm the findings, I would go no further, the reading would be over. The person would need to determine if what I had said was true before returning to see me.

I found that at least a quarter of my clients could not remember much detail of their lives before the age of fifteen. Many would need to ask family members or find photographs for the proof they needed.

You should never feel bad about testing a psychic or being tested. Just like spirits, humans should be tested. If they are speaking the truth, they will never become angry, and all their findings will be true. Why would you want anything less than perfect accuracy when listening to someone predicting your future?

In the rules of energy, remember, intent is 100% of the game.

Be careful what you are thinking when working with someone:

- ✓ Do not have a preconceived notion of your client's intent for the session, be that emotional, spiritual, mental, or physical.
- ✓ Let the client tell you what his/her needs are.
- ✓ Learn to listen: your client will tell you either verbally, or with body language what he/she needs from you. Remember, this is the client's session and he/she may need to go through his/her pain to learn a valuable lesson or to learn that death is also a healing.
- ✓ Make sure you are a clear vessel, meaning clear yourself of your own issues so that your energy vessel is not murky with your own garbage.
- ✓ The responsibility of healing is the clients.
- ✓ Empower clients; teach them how to help themselves. This may be with "homework" – recommendations for such practices as meditation of affirmations.
- ✓ Perfection is one of the hardest things to master. Do not let your ego (good or bad) get in the way of your energy work.

There are many people that believe there is no such thing as coincidence, but that everything happens for a reason. All you can do is your best - the rest is up to the client and creator.

Once you have read this manual over, probably many more times than once, you will be ready to proceed. Remember that there are many ways to work with clients. In this section, we will look at information sessions and readings.

SYMBOLISM

Please refer to Appendices III (Suggested Readings and Internet Resources) for sources of additional information on the symbols.

Interpretation of a symbol on a Rider deck tarot card:

Butterfly	immortality of the soul
Birds	thoughts or inspiration
Castle	dreams
Colors	pay attention to the colors in the card. (See "colors" in the section on Auras.)
Clouds	stormy
Crown	attainment and mastery
Dog	friend
Infinity sign	spiritual
Fish	spiritual
Flames	spirit
Gold	intense, activating, enhancing, attention
Grapes	abundance
Lamp	spiritual light and wisdom
Leaves	growth
Lily/White flowers	pure thoughts, innocence
Lightning	no control
Mountains	bumpy or rough times/obstacles
Pomegranates	female or passive
Roses	desire
Scales	balance

Salamander	fire
Silver	sedating, calming, neutral, friendship, peace, grounding, angels
Square □	first stage of initiation has been completed
Square (with a triangle in it)	second stage
Snake	wisdom
Staff	power, authority, support
Stars	material and spiritual trinity
Sun	better times ahead
Sunflower	radiant energy
Towerman's	creation or personality
Veil	hidden things
Water (calm)	calm times
Water (rough)	rough times
Wheat	abundance
White wands	the same in heaven as on Earth
Wreath	victory

Dream books are a great tool to interpret symbols. Sigmund Freud was also great at interpreting dreams, he said you are all parts of the dream, look at each piece separately and then create the connection.

Trust your gut instincts, what does it mean to you.

Tea Leaf Reading

𝕷et's start you with something easy. Have you ever stared at the clouds? What did you see? Shapes that resembled people, places, or things.

That is how easy Tea leaf reading is. It is the loose-leaf tea leaves that are at the bottom of the cup after the person has finished the tea that are read. The reader stares at the leaves to see the patterns and shapes they make. The symbolism is used as you would in dream interpretation, each symbol is a representation for something, and everything translates into an emotion.

As a Reader, we are going for the emotional attachment. Intuition is reading symbols and interpreting them into emotions.

PROPHECY READINGS

These techniques are used to get more information.

Reading Exercise #1 - For A Lost Items

1. Take a breath
2. Focus and ask up, "Where is the lost _____?, Where can he/she find it?"
3. Say whatever the first image, feeling, knowing, or word is that comes to you.
4. You can always ask up for more information. (You might not always get more, sometimes the item is not to be found).

Reading Exercise #1 - Using Automatic Writing

1. Take a breath.
2. Write the question.
3. Focus your attention up and ask for anyone with integrity and truth to help you with this question.
4. Allow the answer to flow down through your crown chakra and into your writing hand.
5. Start to write the question a second time and record any information following it.
6. Thank the energy when done.

Reading Exercise #3 - Using A Pendulum

(TO RECEIVE A 'YES' OR 'NO' ANSWER)

Always ask if you are "on" and if you can answer the questions. If yes:

1. Have client say his/her question out loud.
2. Take a breath and clear your mind.
3. Saying, "With integrity and honesty," swing the pendulum.
4. Answer the question.
5. Repeat, until all questions are asked and answered.

Reading Exercise #4 - Using Remote Viewing

This is most often used to find a lost or missing person.

1. Take a breath.
2. Focus your energy on the person.
3. Ask up where this person can be found.
4. Write or say the first thing that comes into your mind.
5. You can always ask up more specific questions.
6. Thank the energy after you are finished.

Reading Exercise #5 - Using Sci Scan or Body Scan

To scan a person's health:

1. Take a breath.
2. Relax and focus your attention on the person's body systems one at a time.
3. Take note of anything unusual or problematic.
4. Let go of the energy with a breath, bringing in white love light energy when you are finished.

Reading Exercise #6 - Using Astral Travel

This is most often used to go somewhere to visit or to check it out.

1. Take a breath.
2. Focus on the location.
3. Imagine the place or go up through your crown chakra.
4. Take note of what it looks, feels or sounds like,
5. When finished, wiggle your toes and take a breath.

PROPHECY SESSIONS

Reading Exercise #7 - Using Your Psychic Energy

(I usually tape record my readings and have a clip board with some blank paper, a pen and pendulum handy.)

1. Greet your client and seat him/her across from you.
2. Take a breath and focus your energy and attention on your client. If there is more than one person with you, or the client is very nervous, you might need to start with psychometry to gain the client's information.
3. Make a mental note of anything you already know about this person, what he/she was like when you made the appointment, what might have happened when he/she walked into your office or space. Even something insignificant might be a sign of his/her energy.
    - *Once a lady came for a reading and just as she entered the building, the phone rang. I answered it and nodded at her. (She didn't see the nod because she had started to look at some books and gift items). A moment later a second person walked in and wanted to quickly ask me something. I could not be rude to either the person on the telephone or the person who had come in with a question, so it was about seven minutes before we entered the room for the reading. Just after we sat down, I asked her if she felt that she was ignored in life and not seen as very important. She replied, "Oh, yes - that happens to me all the time."*

4. <u>Always</u> start with a client's past life, meaning <u>this</u> lifetime's past, the client's childhood. Tell him/her detailed information about his/her past, starting at about age five, then ten, fifteen, twenty... Finish at an age about five to ten years younger than the client is today.
5. Go into as much detail as possible on each age. Focus on a specific moment and tell the client about it - what he/she looked like, was wearing, others who were there, what the surroundings were like, his/her feelings, and anything else that you might have noticed.
6. Then move into the present (*which, to me, is within the last year*) and do the same as in Step 5.
7. If you have <u>98%</u> or better of the combined information correct, continue on to the future and then, once again, do the same as in Step 5.
8. Additionally, you may wish to go into a client's past "past life" (before this lifetime).
9. After each section (past, present, future and past life) write the information you gathered on a piece of paper <u>exactly</u> as you said it, asking the client if it is correct. (*I **<u>NEVER</u>** change anything once I have said it, even if the client says. "No, I do not think so." Many, many times I have had a client come back to me saying, "You were right. I found a picture of myself confirming what you said."*).
10. Qualities of a good reading: make sure you are giving guidance, direction, confirmation, encouragement, and life potential; clients come to you for help. They usually want to change something in their lives or have a question answered.
11. Ask the client if he/she has any questions that he/she would like answered. And answer those questions if you can. If you cannot, say so.
12. **<u>ALWAYS</u>** end the session **positively**. Even if there is some negative information, ask up to your angels for what other paths the client can take and what the other paths

would be like.

*Clients hate the practitioner to *"fish"* (using phrases like did you?... was there?... do you remember?), *preach* (telling them what to do), or *having subjective views* (your opinion).

Part of the secret is to ask yourself questions: What does he/she look like? Where is the client? What height is the client? Who is with the client? Are there any animals around? How is he or she feeling? What kind of a child was the client? How was he/she in school? Was there a girl/boyfriend? Did he/she marry?

> *I only had the client pay if I could "get" his/her energy and could usually determine in ten minutes if I was successful. And if I had all "no's" about the client's early childhood and the second or third age, I would end the reading. The client could return if he/she wanted or when they confirmed what I had said. I never want to tell someone information that they might only be a fifty-fifty chance it was incorrect.*

All readings that I do, I read in the same manner as in a psychic reading: past, present, future and past life.

Reading Exercise #8 - Using A Telephone or The Internet

This is like psychic energy reading, the only difference being that the person communicates with you on a telephone or computer.
1. To make a connection to a client's energy, take a breath and send your energy and thoughts through the telephone or computer. Then proceed as you would in person.

Reading Exercise #9 - Using Psychometry

1. Take a breath
2. Hold on to the (item, picture, or handwriting)
3. Speak or write whatever comes.

Reading Exercise #10 - Using Aura Art

1. Take a breath
2. Have the client in mind
3. Start to draw the client's energy.
4. Read the colors, symbols, or anything else that appears.
5. Every time you change your focus, the picture will read differently (for example, money, love, work, relationship, health, children).

Reading Exercise #11 - Using Tarot Card

1. Take a breath
2. Decide which card reading you will be laying out.
3. Have client shuffle the cards or have client in mind when you are shuffling the cards.
4. Read the cards.

Every time you change your focus the cards will read differently (for example, money, love, work, relationship, health, or children).

TAROT CARD READING

The tarot is defined as a set of playing cards. True tarot is symbolism, a sign or object accepted as recalling, typifying or representing a thing, quality or idea.

Dr. Arthur Edward Waite wrote in *The Key to the Tarot*:

"The true tarot is symbolism; it speaks no other language and offers no other sign."

Historical Perspective

The origin of tarot is somewhat ambiguous and is the topic of many researchers who have tried to trace its roots and the reasons for it popularity for psychics, spiritualists and adherents of intuitive practices.

It is generally accepted that tarot first surfaced in Europe in the 15th century as a set of 3 decks called "Visconti Trumps" played by nobles, and from there evolved into tools of divination. Antoine Court de Gebelin is thought to have brought about the "rebirth" of tarot in the 18th century, postulating that they were attributable to Thoth, the Egyptian god of inspired written knowledge, and that they represented historical and mythical knowledge of Egypt. It is believed that the gypsies carried the tarot cards throughout Europe as these nomads were thought to be descendants of the Egyptians.

"Papus" (Dr. Gerald Encausse), a leading French occultist is quoted as saying:

> "...The gypsy...has given us the key which enables us to explain all the symbolism
>
> of the ages... In it, where a man of the people sees only the key to an obscure tradition,
>
> (are) discovered the mysterious links which unite God, the universe and man."

Legends abound regarding documentation of its ancient use. The following are examples:

- When the Christian persecutions were happening with the pagan cults, the Hierophants (priests of the Eleusinian mysteries) handed down their ancestral knowledge to the gypsies, who only re-taught it to those whom they thought were worthy.
- It was also said that the gypsies had been entrusted with the knowledge from the Gnostics, the Montanists and the Manichaeans, as well as the Albigenses.
- There is also a reported relationship with the mysteries of the Jewish Kabalah, as well as those of the Masonic order.
- One of the greatest stories is that when the library at Alexandria was destroyed, the city of Fez became the intellectual capital of the world, to which many wise men flocked. Needing to create a common language, they composed a picture book copious in mystic symbols. Meanings of these signs were passed down verbally from generation to generation

At approximately the same time that Gebelin was making known his theories of the Egyptian origin, Jean-Baptiste Alliette (commonly known as Ettilla) published the first divination interpretation.

Tarot remained an element of occult until Arthur Edward Waite is said to have inspired the next "rebirth" of the tarot in the 20th century. He commissioned Pamela Coleman Smith to create what Waite called the "rectified" tarot: she was the first to add "pips" to the tarot of the Minor Arcana and it is her basic design which is commonly used today.

The deck of tarot used in most readings is that termed the "Rider Waite" but there is a diverse range of standard decks available – some are constructed to be ethereal, some intriguing, others provocative. The deck used is either the choice of the reader, the person whose tarot is being read or the particular situation at the time: in fact, many readers have a variety of decks.

Whatever its history, the tarot remains a phenomenon which is believed by its adherents to be a spiritual tool in guiding and predicting the many aspects of the human existence.

Versions of the deck are manifold and have evolved over the centuries. In the earliest days in Europe, the nobles selected their own Major Arcana cards; these were used as "trump" cards. And, at other times, there were as many as 140 cards in deck. It now widely accepted that a standard tarot deck consists of 78 cards – 22 **High** or **Major Arcana** and 56 **Low** or **Minor Arcana**.

There are similarities between a standard tarot deck and a common deck of playing cards through the cards of the Minor Arcana. With the exception of the "Page", all are represented in the common deck: Ace, 2 – 10, Jack, Queen and King. The only tarot of the Major Arcana which will be found is the "Fool", represented as the "Joker".

Similarly, the suits of the two decks are correlated:

- Hearts = Cups
- Diamonds = Pentacles
- Clubs = Wands
- Spades = Swords

Numbers

Numerology is the parascience that studies the purported mystical or esoteric relationship between numbers and the character or action of physical objects and living things.

Numerology and numerological divination were popular among early mathematicians such as Pythagoras but are no longer considered to be part of modern-day mathematics and are now regarded as pseudo mathematics by most mathematicians. Numerologists often apply distinct definitions to individual digits. These definitions and the resulting permutations between individual digits, or in a mathematical equation, will result in multi-fold meanings.

Today numerology is associated with the *Occult*, alongside Astrology and similar divinatory arts. This is similar to the historical development of astronomy from astrology, and that of chemistry from alchemy. (Source: http://en.wikipedia.org/wiki/Numerology)

Yes or No Readings

Sometimes you will be asked by a client to provide "Yes" or "No" readings. The cards played will give the answer:
Good or happy cards = Yes
Major arcana cards = Yes
Bad or sad cards = No

Numbering –
Roman Numerals 1-100

1= I	1	11 = XI	10+1	30 = XXX	10+10+10
2 = II	1+1	12 = XII	10+1+1	40 = XL	10-50
3 = III	1+1+1	13 = XIII	10+1+1+1	50 = L	50
4 = IV	1-5	14 = XIV	10-1+5	60 = LX	50+10
5 = V	5	15 = XV	10+5	70 = LXX	50+10+10
6 = VI	5+1	16 = XVI	10+5+1	80 = LXXX	50+10+10+10
7 = VII	5+1+1	17 = XVII	10+5+1+1	90 = XC	10-100
8 = VIII	5+1+1+1	18 = XVIII	10+5+1+1+1	100 = C	100
9 = IX	1-10	19 = XIX	10-1+10		
10 = X	10	20 = XX	10+10		

Just as in a regular card deck, the higher and lower arcana in the tarot deck have a numeric value.
Example:
    Ace = 1
    Ace I = 1

Time

The number on the card and the particular suit will give you a time frame for referencing your interpretation.

For example, the VII of Pentacles means that the time frame is 7 months.

    Swords   indicates HOURS
    Cups   indicates DAYS
    Pentacles   indicates MONTHS
    Wands   indicates YEARS

Reading the Cards

It must be emphasized that the basis of tarot is symbolism. The "picture" on each tarot carries associated meanings but how they are "read" will be determined by the reader and the client. It is the reader's interpretation of those symbols based on his/her intuition which will promote a successful reading. The standard interpretation of those symbols is the next section. (Remember that how those interpretations form a "picture" of/for the client is the responsibility of the reader).

I like my students to learn on 'The Rider Tarot Deck' ISBN# 0-913866-13-X.

*High/Major Arcana cards mean what the Spirit World wants you to know.

*Lower/Minor Arcana cards mean what is happen to you on Earth.

- Cups symbolize your emotions
- Pentacles symbolize your materialistic values
- Wands symbolize how you communicate
- Swords symbolize your actions

The Deck - The High/Major Arcana

Any of these 22 cards symbolizes Spiritual Guidance for empowering your soul. These cards also represent your inner self realizing your higher purpose, starting with the Fool card (naïve and open to new experiences) proceeding along your path in life all the way to the World card (success, fulfilment, and ready for a new journey).

(These "Quick Interpretations" are ascribed to Norma Cowie)

#	Higher Arcana	Quick Interpretation
0	Fool	completes all motion by faith
I	Magician	all things are possible
II	High Priestess	choice
III	Empress	abundance
IV	Emperor	experience
V	Hierophant	seeking guidance
VI	Lovers	indecision, confusion
VII	Chariot	drive
VIII	Strength	strength to overcome
IX	Hermit	knowledge needed
X	Wheel of Fortune	action
XI	Justice	what you put out or you get back
XII	Hanged Man	acceptance or reversals
XIII	Death	rebirth from old conditions

XIV	Temperance	blending of all circumstances to create balance
XV	Devil	beware of emotions
XVI	Tower	unexpected events
XVII	Star	knowledge being given out
XVIII	Moon	watch motives
XIX	Sun	growth, rewarding, truth and progress
XX	Judgment	accepting results of one's decision
XXI	The World	attainment

** Card #0 may be the first or the last of the High/Major Arcana

The number of the High/Major Arcana cards indicates laws and lessons, major events or significant changes or influences in the client's life. These should never be ignored, as they tend to weigh more heavily in a reading than those cards of the Minor Arcana. Often these influences are guided or predestined and indicate a period in a person's life over which he or she has little, if any, control.

If you have the following number of High/Major Arcana card(s) in the reading it means:
1. a new beginning or choice
2. the person is in a passive phase and is not to take action; indicates receptivity,
3. union, balance
4. flow and harmony, creativity
5. focus and structure, is a stable period in the person's life, stability, work
6. conflict, chaos, change, challenge; a turbulent time with many ups and downs
7. a peak period, a time of self-expression - very significant; domestic success
8. an initiation of some sort is taking place, evolvement, personal change (like that of attitude, viewpoints, aloneness, or introspection)
9. an extremely important time in a person's life, a time of change and karmic adjustment, Karma, business, money and passion
10. wisdom, completion and endings

Major Arcana or more is a very rare occurrence, and signifies a time of magical occurrences and manifestations, complete alteration in a person's life, significant spiritual intervention (miracles). Perhaps the person, he or she, is a master on the path of enlightenment

Spiritual or Attitude Interpretations/Symbolism of the High/Major Arcana

The Fool 0
Positive: spontaneity, the child within, playfulness, faith, exploration of infinite possibilities, choices, abundance of energy.

Negative: feeling foolish, self-consciousness, foolhardy, lack of faith, promiscuity, acting without thinking of the consequences, bravado, arrogance.

The Magician I
Positive: action, ability to manifest and create, having the ability to realize ideas and dreams, empowerment, the ego, the self, the will; outward expression and using one's power for the good.

Negative: abuse of power, trickery, struggle with the ego, strong use of force, possible violence, uncontrolled Mars energy, overdoing things slightly, can indicate problems with outwardly manifesting one's power in the world.

The High Priestess II
Positive: receptivity, female energy, fluidity, psychic and creative ability, secrets and mystery; the perfect female men dream about; openness; she shows that one knows what one needs; dreams and visions, intuition, the perfect wife or girlfriend.

Negative: fear or uncertainty about intuition or psychic impression, keeping secrets though this may hurt someone; sneakiness, promiscuity, cheating, unwarranted flirtation, leading a secret life, occult, abuse of psychic ability, unethical.

The Emperor III
Positive: leadership, authority, the father figure, responsibility, stability, making decisions unclouded by emotion, fairness; business, firm or corporation, government; left brain activity, facts and figures, stricture, masculinity.

Negative: fear of using too much power, egotistical, abusing power, uncaring, unfeeling, selfishness, the macho man, arrogance, critical of self and others, low self-esteem, stubbornness.

The Empress IV
Positive: fertility, sex appeal, motherhood, pregnancy, sexuality, sensuality abundance, growth, generosity, nurturing self and others, femininity, prosperity, the Mother Earth, the perfect wife or lover, sharing and caring, sensitivity, growth and all growing things, manager of the heart.

Negative: abuse of sexuality, victim of sexual abuse, false charms, the nymphomaniac or woman of ill repute, famine or hard times, selfishness in an emotional or physical sense, calculating and scheming, insecurity, grasping selfishly at love, jealousy.

The Hierophant V
Positive: teaching or learning, the social structure, priesthood, manmade religion, dogma or doctrine, church, society, school, can indicate groups of people believing in the same thing, the upright citizen, organizations; psychic control exercised by mostly male authority figures in our society (doctors, judges, psychiatrists); conventional, worthy, doing that which pleases others rather than the self, trying to fit in with a group, organization or certain structure or behavior, marriage in the conventional sense.

Negative: going against the grain or the norm, following one's own drummer, struggle to overcome conditioning in stereotypical upbringing, unconventional beliefs or behavior, often a loner, unpopularity, oddity, occult beliefs, the supernatural or unknown.

The Lovers VI
Positive: relationship or marriage, true love and passion, choices (usually of an emotional nature), friendship, the couple, sexuality, attraction of physical or emotional nature, choice between physical or emotional love.

Negative: a love triangle, unfaithfulness, wrong choices usually leading to heartache and despair, falling in love for all the wrong reasons, abandonment of self or others, a break-up between people in love.

The Chariot VII

Positive: leadership, attainment of goals, success, conquest and victory, gaining control over emotional or physical issues, keeping it together, strength, vibrant energy, movement, possible move or travel, someone who is very active and nearly tireless, motion.

Negative: the male flirt, short-term lover, conquest and victory over others, sexual conquest without emotional attachment, kit of emotional entanglements, selfishness, someone who is overbearing or controlling, vehicular trouble, uncontrolled emotions, anger and temper tantrums, the base nature, primal instinct, no forethought to consequences.

Strength VIII

Positive: love is stronger than hate, courage in the face of all enemies, the diplomat, fearlessness, bravery, heroism, the higher nature, compassion, attraction, extra strength in reserve, hidden powers coming to the surface in time of need, fearless use of one's power, self-confidence, sympathy, Kundalini energy.

Negative: lust, depression, feeling powerless and helpless, vindictiveness, insecurity, fear and doubts, illness, fear of wanting too much, holding back, inappropriate use of power; *for a man* — fear of a woman's power, *for a woman* — fear of a man's power; the need to develop inner strength.

The Hermit IX
Positive: knowing one's path, wisdom, knowledge, experience, often an older or more mature person who offers valid advice, solitude, introspection, getting to know oneself, someone from the past may be indicated, reunion.

Negative: loneliness, depression, lacking wisdom, refusal to take advice, refusal to learn or grow up, immaturity, mourning lost youth.

Wheel of Fortune X
Positive: destiny is taking place, luck breaking old and outworn patterns, the cycle of life, big changes coming, a twist of fate, good fortune.

Negative: ill luck, a time in a person's life which feels miserable and difficult, fighting destiny, obstacles.

Justice XI
Positive: fairness in dealings, balance, karmic balance usually indicated by some change, sometimes indicates legal matters, courts, lawyers, large institutions, companies, government, jails.

Negative: unfairness in dealings, negative Karma, imbalance, what goes around comes around, what you send out comes back to you.

The Hanged Man XII
Positive: surrender to higher forces, Karmic cleansing, giving up the ego and letting go, feeling closer to spirit and spiritual guidance, meditation upon that which cannot be seen but is felt, a waiting period, a time of "not knowing" but sensing.

Negative: hanging in limbo, feelings of stagnation, standstill in one's affairs, fighting against one's destiny...though to no avail. (This is a difficult energy in a person's life; often the person cannot help but resist that which is to be, especially in relationships, a strong need for compassion and acceptance is indicated here, need lots of patience).

Death XIII
Positive: a big change coming into a person's life, the change is always notable and final, often brings with it physical change as well, such as a move, a new beginning in another direction, a final transition; it can indicate a physical death, depending on the other cards in the reading, but it is unethical to predict death to anyone. (**Never predict death to anyone!** You could be wrong and cause unnecessary anxiety and stress. Tell the person, instead, that the old way of life is on its way out and a new one is about to begin).

Negative: fear of death, fear of change, not wanting something to end, such as a relationship or job, can indicate that the person really wants things to change, but that the change is not possible at this time, can indicate a very slow "death"; ultimately the person must let go, grieve and move on.

Temperance XIV
Positive: spiritual guidance, compatibility with another person place or thing, successful ingredients, victory on an emotional or psychic plane, gaining balance and equilibrium in the face of difficulties, potential disturbance, mastering oneself, integration of the opposites of one's nature, becoming one by merging the positive with the negative side of one's nature, harmony, can also indicate the merging of two souls such as in a relationship of soul mates, can also indicate medication that will benefit the person.

Negative: a chaotic time of imbalance, crying over spilled milk, inability to remain in control of the self, temper tantrums, medication or drugs that are not beneficial, drug abuse, alcohol abuse, abuse of self and others, destructive behavior or circumstances.

The Devil XV
Positive: the devil becomes positive when reversed, for it indicates the ability to remove the chains or bonds that are holding the person; it indicates positive mastery over the self and the ability to remove oneself from negative situations or people; there is healing available here.

Negative: in its natural position, the Devil indicates supreme negativity, the dark side of one's nature; all negative emotions, such as rage, uncontrolled anger, jealousy, fear, hatred and scorn, are indicated here; can indicate black magic and the negative side of the Occult, addiction to drugs, alcohol or even negative thought, addiction to sex, the dark side of sexuality, frigidity or perversity, vindictiveness, vengefulness, uncontrolled passions usually accompanied by insecurity and self-loathing.

The Tower XVI
Positive: There is not really a positive side to this card. It almost always indicates a sudden, sometimes unexpected, physical change or disruption such as bankruptcy, a disaster such as a flood or an Earthquake, an accident, or the like. It can even indicate sudden and unexpected news which will most certainly affect the person's life in a profound way like the loss of a job, or the loss of a relationship. Often there is some kind of betrayal indicated in a relationship, something that will cause loss of trust or even affection. In a world situation it could indicate a war or natural disasters. Usually the past gets severed from the future, bringing complete and utter change. Depression and despair often accompany this card.

Negative: disruption and change, trying to hold back the changes to keep them from overwhelming the person, to slow the change, to make the change less disruptive.

The Star XVII
Positive: dreams, hopes, inspiration, psychic intuition, precognitive dreams or feelings, the calm after the storm, a period of grace, a healing time, recovery after illness, sometimes indicates openness and trust, growth of psychic abilities; this card brings the exact opposite of the Tower card; peace, tranquility, calm, love and the opening of the heart chakra, Spiritual growth and evolution. (As the card representing the person being read for, it indicates very strong healing ability, healing hands - also a card of prayer and communion with the divine.)

Negative: not believing that the healing energy is available, needless suffering and doubt, a need to open oneself to spirit and to love, a need to accept the positive energies into one's life.

The Moon XVIII
Positive: psychic ability, trying to divine answers that remain unclear, energies of the moon which affects the tides, receptivity, attempting to mend one's ways, often the Moon works on a subconscious level indicating inner transformation, a feeling of being guided in some direction though the purpose remains unclear.

Negative: intuition is blocked completely, deception by self or others, possible danger to self or someone you know, keep eyes open to avert the danger.

The Sun XIX

Positive: happiness and joy, innocence, children or could indicate the inner child, warm, sun-filled days ahead, courage, being at one's best, surrounded by positive energy, ability to bring happiness and joy to others, sharing and caring, pleasure in expressing one's uniqueness and individuality, creativity.

Negative: happiness and joy will once again come into the person's life, even if things do not look that way for the moment; some hardship indicated, but this card assures the person that this too shall pass and good times will reign again; could mean that something that is offered is "too good to be true."

Judgment XX

Positive: enlightenment, the dawn after the darkness, seeing things clearly, sound judgment on matters, fairness, the Universal healing power that is available to us all, a transformation that liberates, a big change has happened and some decisions have been made for the better, spiritual intervention into the person's life (sometimes with the person being aware of this but sometimes not).

Negative: some negative judgment has been made either by the person or against the person, sometimes this negative judgment is made against the self; uncertainty, feeling lost, helplessness.

The World XXI

Positive: attainment, completion of a cycle; turning over a new leaf, success; moving on with one's life; sometimes indicates a physical move; journey, often a long-distance move; self-acceptance; the old path is done and a doorway stands open toward something new and often untried; endless possibilities to be explored.

Negative: not seeing the doorway to the new, blinded by confusing thoughts and doubts; not ready to move on with one's life, not believing that a cycle is done and over, hanging on to something obsolete; fear of the unknown, holding back the changes.

The Low/Minor Arcana

Following are the individual card meanings of the Lower Arcana suits: wands, pentacles, swords, and cups. Each 'suit' has a unique symbolism meaning for each number. Check the description of each card separately! The Lower Arcana symbolizes Emotional, Mental, and Physical Guidance for empowering your body and mind.

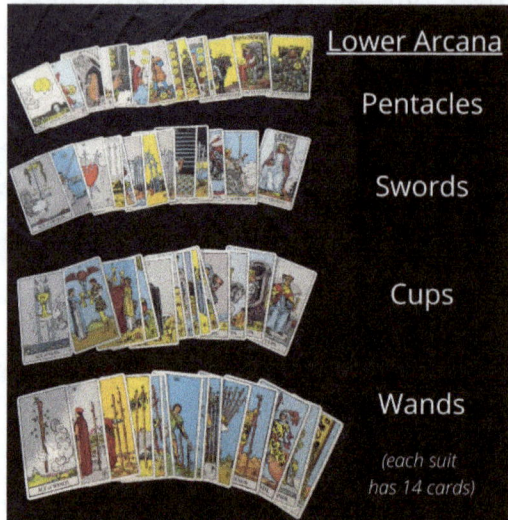

NOTE:
- ➢ All cards with in the 'WANDS' suit take on a COMMUNICATION theme, focus, or symbolism.

- ➢ All cards with in the 'CUPS' suit take on an EMOTIONAL theme, focus, or symbolism.
- ➢ All cards with in the 'SWORDS' suit take on an ACTION theme or symbolism.
- ➢ All cards with in the 'PENTACLES' suit take on a MATERIALISTIC/FINANCIAL theme, focus, or symbolism.

General condition of your LIFE, at this moment in time.
Remember you can change your blueprint!

Wands = Clubs

Physical mind -	Your ideas, thoughts, communication
Emotional -	Drives, passions, enthusiasm, energy, and action
Astrological sign -	Leo, Aries, Sagittarius
Fire sign	
Audio	

Ace I: New ideas
Symbolizes: pens, letter, written word, new creativity, new beginnings, perhaps of an enterprise; a new start in relationships; penis, sexual activity, fertility, renewal of the self, passion, energy

Two II: Contemplating Your Idea
Symbolizes: partnership in the making, plans on the verge of being implemented, intuition and sense of the energy within, drive, seeing the whole world unfold before you

Three III: Putting Thoughts Into Action
Symbolizes: creating something, material results, active flow, putting plans into action, creative energy, seeing your ship come in, work coming in, rewards for labor expended, harvest, communication

Four IV: Ideas Firmly Established
Symbolizes: celebration, marriage or anniversary, unions or reunions with family or friends, feelings of happiness, relationship, boundaries within a relationship, social structure, stability, joy

Five V: Confusion of Ideas
Symbolizes: challenge, active struggle, competition, power struggles; could be arguments of either a friendly or unfriendly nature

Six VI: Victory is Assured
Symbolizes: leadership, winning, victory, success, active expression of energy; a "yes" card

Seven VII: Unsure of Ideas
Symbolizes: struggle followed by victory; ability to cope, overcoming challenges, feeling alone yet able to handle adversity efficiently, getting by without the help of others

Eight VIII: Ideas Will Soon Materialize
Symbolizes: a happy card: movements, flight, change of residence or journey, arrows of love, enjoying the out of doors, renewed energy, a good time for taking initiative, courage, swiftness of events and happenings, unexpected meetings, communication, travel, success, money, passion

Nine IX: Defending Ideas
Symbolizes: defensiveness, a long difficult process of events in which one has suffered but retained enough energy to get things done or to make changes, sensitivity and guardedness, a cycle of events has ended and a new cycle is at hand, protecting, hard to hang on to what one has, liable to lose something but it won't be a big deal

Ten X: Too Many Ideas
Symbolizes: burdens and pressures, stress, possible change of residence, worry and anxiety, feeling scattered, too many irons in the fire, weighed down

Page: Contemplating New Thoughts
Symbolizes: news, birth, children, communication, uninhibited personality, musician type person, playfulness, joy, message, phone call, gifted in music, female baby

Knight: Putting Ideas into Action
Symbolizes: movement, flight, a loyal young man, somewhat immature, friendship and loyalty, transportation, spontaneity, flirtation, the life of the

party, a tease, flamboyant, change, moody, passionate, good lover, male baby

Queen: Tendency to be Sidetracked from Goals because of Emotions
Symbolizes: leader, a fire sign (Aries, Leo or Sagittarius), a woman who is mature and confident, possesses healing energy, kind and generous, dignified and goes after what she wants with purpose, usually fair in coloring but not always, a woman full of energy and drive who speaks her mind and is courageous and fearless; possibly a lesbian, blond, tall, athletic, large boned

King: Projecting Ideas
Symbolizes: leader, often a businessman or someone self-employed; positive father figure, friendly supportive and understanding personality; sees problems and can help to solve them; caring and efficient, factual, though is intuitive and good at reading people; steadfast and responsible and able to handle a crisis without falling apart; somewhat proud and can be hot-tempered and arrogant in his negative aspect; usually a good lover, responsible, likes to work for himself, creative, great ideas, attractive, reading, writing, music and dancing; well-built and gets noticed.

Cups = Hearts

Physical mind -	Emotions
Emotional -	How you feel, values/emotions Pure emotions, love
Astrological sign -	Pisces, Cancer, Scorpio
Water sign	
Feeler	

Ace I: New Attitude Brings Reward
Symbolizes: new love, overflowing of the spirit, new relationships possible; falling in love with either the self or others, learning to love, words of love from an admirer, warmth, growth, marriage, gifts of the spirit

Two II: Communication
Symbolizes: a couple, toasting to love, romance, relationship, close friendship, partnership, commitment, honeymoon stage, physical love, plans to be together

Three III: Happiness
Symbolizes: celebration or good times shared with friends, fun and harmless gossip, parties, heart to heart sharing of news, friends reuniting, friendship

Four IV: Be More Aware of What Is Occurring
Symbolizes: rejection, possibly of an offer, something being offered or served (such as a drink); on the negative side it can mean indulgence of alcoholic beverages, extreme depression, wanting to be left alone, boredom, the zest for life seems to be gone, sadness, closed off, meditation

Five V: Crying Over Past Events
Symbolizes: loss, sadness, regrets, sorrow with something left over; perhaps the relationship can be saved by the right action; loss but an important personal lesson may have been learned from this loss; crying over what is lost, not seeing what one still has, need to let go

Six VI: Happy Memories of the Past
Symbolizes: reunions, someone from the past returning, childhood memories or friends from the past; family memories, longing for something or someone from the past, clinging to memories, gifts, children issues

Seven VII: Imagination At Work
Symbolizes: dreams, illusions, fantasy, can indicate drugs or alcohol-induced visions, visions though somewhat clouded, choices, warning to take care to make the right choice; opportunity, but be careful to look at the

opportunities to see if they are valid: one is the right one, the others are false

Eight VIII: Leaving What You Know and Going
Symbolizes: walking away from emotional issues or things previously held dear; moving, choosing a different path in life, seeking enlightenment; bravely walking toward the unknown, taking chances, trying something new, relationship break up, travel

Nine IX: Contentment and Satisfaction
Symbolizes: fulfillment, satisfaction, satiation, wish fulfillment, pleasures of the senses, sexuality, gratification, gifts and wishes coming true, manifestation of a dream, emotional satisfaction

Ten X: Happiness and Content for Everyone
Symbolizes: marriage, family, the ultimate feelings that love can bring, commitment, passion, union, marital vows and promises, dreams coming true

Page: Surprises in Life
Symbolizes: romance and flirtation, maybe teasing, a relationship in the making though it will take time to bloom and mature; innocent friendship may turn to love, though not right away; fertility, pregnancy, birth, a child (usually a girl), gifts, joyful or uplifting news, creative, writer, artist

Knight: Proceeding Slowly and Surely Ahead
Symbolizes: a typical Sir Galahad: romantic young man, lover, somewhat immature, sexual prowess, passion,

masculinity; romantic opportunity, usually a very good-looking man, sex appeal, stamina, emotional change, journey, play with your emotions, roaming eye, can't be totally trusted

Queen: Too Much Imagination
Symbolizes: a sensuous woman, somewhat dreamy, can be somewhat shy and quiet; she is caring, gentle and nurturing and often signifies motherhood, even playing mother to another; she is often psychic or very intuitive and receives much information through dreams or meditation; usually has very intense eyes and/or is fair in coloring, a good lover that most men fantasize about, dependent, sensitive, very feminine, dumb blond, petite, fine boned, great mother, loves animals, may gain weight with age

King: Projecting Ahead into Life
Symbolizes: a very caring and gentle man, often a business man; responsible and willing and able to offer a helping hand; kind and considerate, and often is married; loves children and to play; possesses an emotional nature and is not afraid to show his feelings; very intuitive and able to read people or motives easily; not easily deceived; quiet nature, patient, friendly, family, stay at home kind of man, may be lazy or couch potato, anchor in the storm, early balding, can't easily handle turbulence, loyal, responsible, may gain weight with age.

Swords = Spades

Physical mind -	Mental, Actions
Emotional -	How you deal with problems/challenges, Strife, sharp tongue, conflict, obstacles, communication
Astrological sign -	Libra, Aquarius, Gemini
Air sign	
Knower	

Ace I: Problems Being Solved
Symbolizes: power, new beginnings, the use of power to manifest, sudden changes, sudden passion or romance, sudden outbursts, the power to love or hate, create, or destroy

Two II: Accepting Reality
Symbolizes: an uneasy truce; not willing to see the truth, not willing to listen or accept what is being said or done, has the ability to take off the blinders but refuses to; stubbornness, lack of vision, deliberates inactivity,

desiring peace at any price, turning a "blind eye" to a person or situation, choosing not to hear or see

Three III: Disappointment and Heartbreak
Symbolizes: hurt, heartache, sorrow; loss, usually of affection; can indicate a love triangle or a third-party interfering in a relationship; break up, fear of losing a lover; in health matters it can indicate surgery or heart trouble, chest pains

Four IV: Answer Lies Within
Symbolizes: illness, depression, wanting to be left alone, medication or the need to meditate, boredom, listlessness, feeling miserable; in certain situations, it can be a card of hospitalization or even death depending on the other cards. (However, <u>never</u> prophesy death as it is unethical and would needlessly upset someone as most people fear death. Simply tell the person to use more caution in his/her life and take preventive measures. Use the other cards to divine the circumstance around the situation.)

Five V: Conflict
Symbolizes: anger, cowardice, arguments, frustration, confrontations, sometimes unfair dealings, bitterness and resentment; often warns of a fight about to happen unless preventive measures are taken; betokens a victory, but one that is empty and meaningless such as an act of vengeance

Six VI: Problems Which Will Soon Be Ended
Symbolizes: passage, away from difficulties, not happy, move to get away; there is fear of being overwhelmed, although in most cases the fear is unfounded, slow

progress, clarity and mental keenness, the ability to see the biggest picture; needs to learn to trust in the powers that be (Let go and let God decide is usually the advice that can be given with this card.)

Seven VII: Creating Problems for Yourself
Symbolizes: the card of the thief, not necessarily of material goods, although this is certainly a possibility; dishonesty, with either the self or others, deception, sneakiness and underhanded dealings, (warning - bite your tongue), lies, cheating, dishonest, often the theft is that of peace of mind; cowardliness is indicated.

Eight VIII: Temporary Problems
Symbolizes: entrapment, bondage, feeling trapped in a situation but inability to change the present circumstances; restrictions, sometimes self-imposed; narrow-mindedness and feeling stuck, also means the inability to let go and move on; slander and suffering is also indicated; being controlled by someone or something

Nine IX: Feeling Sorry for Oneself
Symbolizes: overwhelmed, sorrow, sadness, sleeplessness (not being able to sleep at night), sorrow, often indicates a loss or a struggle within, illness, depression, fear of loss; worry or concern over someone, perhaps a loved one but often the fear is unfounded; feelings of being overwhelmed by circumstance or events; could indicate the loss of a loved one due to separation or even death

Ten X: End of Problems
Symbolizes: the ultimate of what strife, hatred or aggression can do; devastation and loss, often accompanied by heartache and sorrows; the good thing about this card is that the worst has happened and now healing is possible; one cannot sink any lower, from here on things can only get better

Page: Defensive
Symbolizes: mistrust, wanting to do things in one's own way, not trusting the advice of others, the need to experience life on one's own terms, no matter the consequences; the typical adolescent; impatience, anger and resentment that may stem from the past or from earlier setbacks and failures; building walls around the self, guardedness, inability to open the heart for fear of pain, emotions are stuck, upsetting messages, person with "chip on one's shoulder"

Knight: Going Too Fast
Symbolizes: an arrogant young man, impetuous and proud, the rational mind, the intellect gets disconnected from emotions or feelings; the unexpected is about to happen, sudden change, outbursts, temper, a quick tongue, quick wit, selfishness, dominance, tyranny

Queen: Watch Out for Defensive Thoughts
Symbolizes: survivor, strength, sharp tongue; a woman who appears to be hard and unfeeling, she has experienced loss at the deepest level, perhaps she is widowed or has lost a child, usually she is alone; she is very intelligent and able to get things done; can be very

critical of others and of the self, being overly judgmental and sometimes hurtful; can be withdrawn and lonely; cold, sad, depressed; usually she blames someone else for her misfortune; has a difficult time giving or receiving any kind of nurturing; possibly dislikes other women, looking upon them as a threat in some way; pain of the heart, can take care of herself, red hair, thinner; if the card represents a man he doesn't think very much of women

King: Defensive and Stubborn
Symbolizes: often a professional type person, such as a lawyer, police, or army officer, can be a doctor; power and control; needs to learn to wield his power with compassion and care; speech and communications; on the negative side, perhaps he is afraid to speak his mind, or perhaps has a very sharp tongue; needs to learn to express himself with sincerity and gentleness; needs to stop fearing his emotional side.

Pentacles = Diamonds

Physical mind -	Physical Body, Materialistic
Emotional -	How you manifest/create or attitudes, Money, lottery, material goods, generosity, value, solid business
Astrological sign -	Taurus, Virgo, Capricorn
Earth sign	
Visual	

Ace I: New Material Conditions
Symbolizes: new money, beginnings of something in the material world, new material goods, anything that can be touched or felt or seen in the physical world, can be a new job, car or furniture; also physical love, such as a new lover, pregnancy, womb; gift, new job, new home, new gains and prosperity

Two II: Try to Balance Material Affairs of Life
Symbolizes: choices, often trying to juggle two things at the same time, maintaining balance in the face of difficulties, can indicate two jobs, two sources of money or income, two projects, twins; meeting more than one need as the same time; if negative there can be some difficulties with juggling two jobs, two relationships or projects

Three III: Aware of Responsibilities
Symbolizes: creativity, reward, perhaps a job offer, new employment or business, recognition for work well done, bonuses, money and earned rewards; in the negative it would indicate the opposite, such as not being recognized for the work being done or not being paid enough

Four IV: Holding On Tightly
Symbolizes: a need for physical space, solitude and quiet; need to take care of the self and say no to everything that is contrary to that; can indicate holding on tightly to money, such as having to budget very carefully; sometimes indicates a person who is miserly and un-giving; can indicate the need to protect the self from an energy drain caused by another

Five V: Out in the Cold
Symbolizes: poverty, tension, high stress and worry, struggle, poverty and its related issues, feelings of being left out in the cold and abandoned; depression can lead to illness, spiritual darkness; hopelessness, lack of faith

Six VI: Having to Put Out

Symbolizes: generosity, gifts and presents, fairness in dealings, having more than enough to share; on the negative side can indicate fear of success, or a feeling there might not be enough to go around, withholding personal energy, paycheck

Seven VII: Keep On...Your Project will be Completed Soon

Symbolizes: a waiting period, gestation, results are not ready to harvest; can indicate a period in a person's life that seems at a standstill; obstacles, frustration, impatience, wishing very hard so manifest quicker tasks, business ideas are not ready yet, money worries

Eight VIII: Working Steadfastly, Beginning New Endeavour

Symbolizes: work and labor, trying to find meaning and reward for one's work, paychecks, hard work for little money, a job offer, trying to find the type of work that is the "right" one; can also mean boredom with current work and a desire to change job or careers; stable, will get a job soon

Nine IX: Contentment and Peace of Mind

Symbolizes: abundance and plenty, independence, financial independence, security; usually the individual is on his or her own, difficulties to be with a loved one because of work, being busy and occupied within career; also indicates creativity and/or healing power; motivation though, on the negative, could indicate the lack thereof; sometimes indicates not finding enough personal space to be creative, writer's block; often a desire to be in the public eye or to go out into the world to earn money rather than to create something at home; content, loner and financial stability

Ten X: Material Success
Symbolizes: abundance, family money, inheritance, family or community support; prosperity within business or enterprise, success; on the negative side, a lack of support from family, friends or community - instead pressures are being added to the individual by family or community; loyalty, new job

Page: Too Absorbed in One Thing
Symbolizes: learning or training for new skills, either formally or informally, reading, writing, letters, news, a child; seeking knowledge, awaiting information, perhaps from the universe (via meditation); vulnerability, sensitivity, being open to receive; negative feelings, childish and insecure, negative childhood memories of being told one was not good enough; also learning to depend upon the universe with trust and faith of a child; student, studying, money

Knight: Sitting Still While Surveying Where He Wants To Go
Symbolizes: very predictable, steadfast, steadily pushes ahead, not much imagination; a young man who is solid and steadfast, reliable and stable, usually works with his hands (labor), does work then goes home, finished his training; he is grounded, meticulous and goal orientated, has confidence in the self and the future; negatively, he

shows fear of failure, disorganization, and inability to believe that success is possible

Queen: Aware of Limitations
Symbolizes: a woman who is abundant and prosperous, often a business type person or someone in the health profession; Virgo, Taurus or Capricorn type temperament; generous and caring, warm and nurturing; someone down to Earth, motherly, the ideal mother; loves cooking, back rubs and physical sexuality; dark haired, heavy set, always giving, knows the value of a dollar, intelligent, generous with gifts; negatively she could be sexually frigid, maybe not liking her own body, feeling shame; maybe feels overworked and is in need of nurturing herself; lack of confidence, a sense of need; needs to learn to love herself

King: Material Attainment
Symbolizes: a businessman, employer or one of wealth or affluence; action and accomplishment in the material world, technical or mechanical skills, abundance, can be someone who is willing to assist, benefactor, man of the world, boss, most men dream of living in luxury; negatively, can be a workaholic or be overworked and tired; there is a feeling of overworking without getting anything accomplished; a feeling of being overwhelmed, can also mean a father who never was around to help with the children (dead-beat-dad).

The Game of Tarot

The cards only answer for the person reading them; meaning that if more than one person at the session knows how to read the cards, the reader is the only one with the correct interpretation.

When you are reading, study the cards, take into account the written information and then <u>trust</u> your first glance, feelings, and thoughts. Always go with your first impression and speak it, then follow up with more detail.

Ideas to the cards - Look at the face card: is it Happy or sad? Is he/she looking into the past, present or future? Is the card grounded? Guarded? Bright colors or dark colors? Moving or standing still?

Traditional Tarot Reading

- Put black velvet, satin, or similar material on top of the table so the cards show up brightly.
- Sit across from the client/seeker.
- Choose which type of Tarot Card Reading you are doing.
- Lightly tap the cards on the table to clear the energy.
- Have the client set their intent and shuffle the cards.

- ➤ Place the cards onto the table, face up (number of cards will depend on the game/arrangement you are playing).
- ➤ Read the cards separately and then together.
- ➤ After you have read the cards, answer any questions the client may have. You may pull more cards to answer some of their questions.

There are many choices of the game or card arrangement that you can choose from, following are my favorites.

Tarot Card Reading Arrangements

I. FULL READING (ABOUT ONE HOUR)

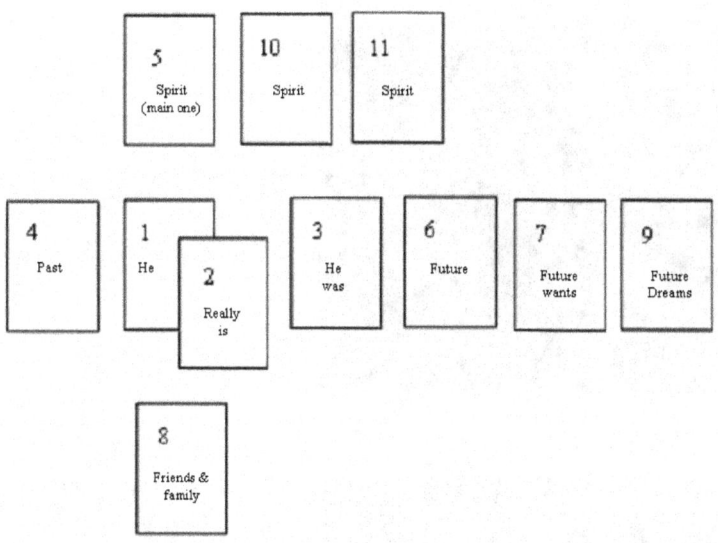

1. Type of person he shows he is (what others see)
2. Type of person he really is (core being)
3. Type of person he was (what people use to see)
4. Past life (usually one year)
5. What life Spirit/Creator wants for him (Main)
6. Future as of today
7. What he wants for the future (What he says he wants)
8. What his friends think of him
9. What his dreams are (what he really wants)
10. What life Spirit/Creator wants for him *(extra information for card 5)*
11. What life Spirit/Creator wants for him *(extra information for card 5)*

Method (start with 1st card position)
1. Read each card one at a time

2. For extra information of each card, place one to the left of each card - Read each new card one at a time for the positive or good meaning.

3. Instead of reading a negative meaning for an upside-down card, place one to the right of each card for the negative or bad meaning.
4. Then read all the cards together.
5. Count how many upper arcana (spiritual meaning) there are in total.
6. Answer any questions using another card, turn a new card over from the deck.

II. FAST, OVERALL READING (15 – 30 MINUTES)

```
  ┌─────┐  ┌─────┐  ┌─────┐
  │  1  │  │  2  │  │  3  │
  │ Past│  │Present│ │Future│
  └─────┘  └─────┘  └─────┘
```

1. Past
2. Present
3. Future

Method:
1. Read each card one at a time
2. Then place one to the left of each card.
   a. Read each new card one at a time for the positive.
   b. Then place one to the right of each card for the negative.
3. Then read all the cards together.
4. Answer any questions.

III. TO ANSWER A QUESTION OR DILEMMA READING (15 – 30 MINUTES)

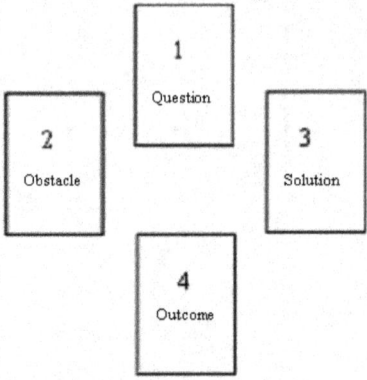

1. Question/Dilemma
2. Obstacle
3. What can help
4. Outcome

Method:
1. Read each card one at a time
2. Then place one to the left of each card.
    a. Read each new card one at a time for the positive
    b. Then place one to the right of each card for the negative.
3. Then read all the cards together.
4. Answer any questions.

Reading Exercise #12 - Astrology

You will need:

- Your date of birth
- Time of birth - for a more accurate reading, you will need your exact time of birth (the chart will still work if you do not have it).
- The American Ephemeris for the 20th & 21st Century by Neil F. Michelson
    - Midnight is great, the day starts at 12:00 am
    - 1900-2000   ISBN 093512719-4
    - and 2000-2050   ISBN 0935127-59-3
- **Or** go on the internet and look up Swiss Ephemeris Year of _(your birth year)___?

Definition (Wiki) - Astrology is based off Astronomy.

Astronomy

Astronomy is the scientific study of celestial objects (such as stars, planets, comets, nebulae, star clusters and galaxies) and phenomena that originate outside the Earth's atmosphere (such as the cosmic background radiation). It is concerned with the evolution, physics, chemistry, meteorology, and motion of celestial objects, as well as the formation and development of the universe.

A good start to this course is to go outside and look up into a clear night's sky.

Astrology:

Astrology is a group of systems, traditions, and beliefs which hold that the relative positions of celestial bodies and related details can provide information about personality, human affairs, and other terrestrial matters. A practitioner of astrology is called an astrologer.

Astrologers believe that the movements and positions of celestial bodies either directly influence life on Earth or correspond to events experienced on a human scale. Modern astrologers define astrology as a symbolic language, an art form, or a form of divination. Despite differences in definitions, a common assumption of astrologers is that celestial placements can aid in the interpretation of past and present events, and the prediction of the future. Astrology is generally considered a pseudoscience or superstition by the scientific community for its inability to demonstrate statistically significant predictions, with psychology explaining much of the continued faith in it a matter of cognitive biases.

Numerous traditions and applications employing astrological concepts have arisen since its earliest recorded beginnings in the 3rd millennium BC. Astrology has played an important role in the shaping of culture, early astronomy, the Vedas, and various disciplines throughout history. In fact, astrology and astronomy were often indistinguishable before the modern era, with the desire for predictive and divinatory knowledge, one of the motivating factors for astronomical observation. Astronomy began to diverge from astrology after a period of gradual separation from the Renaissance up until the 18th century. Eventually, astronomy distinguished itself as the empirical study of astronomical objects and phenomena, without regard to the terrestrial implications of astrology.

The word "astrology" comes from the Latin term astrologia ("astronomy"), which in turn derives from the Greek noun αστρολογία: ἄστρον, astron ("constellation" or "star") and -λογία, -logia ("the study of").

History

Main article: History of astrology

In the 15th-century image from the Très Riches Heures du Duc de Berry showing projected correlations between areas of the body and the zodiacal signs. Many believe that the origins of much of the astrological doctrine and method that would later develop in Asia, Europe, and the Middle East are found among the ancient Babylonians and their system of celestial omens that began to be compiled around the middle of the 2nd millennium BCE.[19] They believe this system of celestial omens later spread, either directly or indirectly through the Babylonians and Assyrians, to other areas such as India, the Middle East, and Greece, where it merged with pre-existing indigenous forms of astrology.[20] Thus, Babylonian astrology migrated to Greece, initially as early as the middle of the 4th century BCE, and then around the late 2nd or early 1st century BCE, after the Alexandrian conquests, this Babylonian astrology was mixed with the Egyptian tradition of decanic astrology to create horoscopic astrology. This new form of astrology, which appears to have originated in Alexandrian Egypt, spread across the ancient world into Europe, the Middle East, and India.

The Horoscope

The 18th-century Icelandic manuscript is showing astrological houses and glyphs for planets and signs. Central to horoscopic astrology and its branches is the calculation of the horoscope or astrological chart. This two-dimensional diagrammatic representation shows the celestial bodies' apparent positions in the heavens from the vantage of a location on Earth at a given time and place. The horoscope is also divided into twelve different celestial houses which govern different areas of life. Calculations performed in casting a horoscope involve arithmetic and simple geometry, which serve to locate the apparent position of heavenly bodies on desired dates and times based on astronomical tables. In ancient Hellenistic astrology the ascendant demarcated the first celestial house of a horoscope. The word for the ascendant in Greek was horoskopos from which horoscope derives. In modern times, the word has come to refer to the astrological chart.

Different types of Astrology

There are many types, Aztec, Japanese, Chinese, etc.

The main two seem to be:
- Western Astrology – Aries Chart / Natal Chart /Tropical Chart
- Vedic (Ayurveda /Eastern) Astrology – Sidereal Chart

*In this book we will be studying Western Astrology

What you can use Astrology for:

Astrology is used mostly for finding out the personalities of a person and is a great tool to use to find out:

- Your Horoscope (most common use)
- If you can work with someone; like a business partner and how you will interact together
- Your children's personalities
- Your soulmate
- It can also be used to determine the best day for an event.
- You can also use astrology for the personality of a business, home, etc. you need its birth date. When did it start up, or when was it built?
  - Did you know a house or business ages like a human (twelve years old, maybe trying to be mature but before its time, etc.)?
- World events

Astrology is like a resume...

> It can tell what you have done (past life) and what you are good at and when the stars (planets) are on your side.

> The value lies in the ability to reveal hidden causes at work in our lives. Astrology shows us our potential, what our work in this life should be, lessons to learn, and why we act a certain way, and why others act another. Astrology charts our path.

Astrology is divided into two parts:

1. **Exoteric/External influences**
   Covers the mundane aspects of life, some examples are: astrology can tell the farmer when planting is most favorable, the sailor when it is best to set sail, the doctor the underlying cause of dis-ease, the teacher the basic nature of their student and all parents the tendencies and capabilities of their child.

2. **Esoteric/Internal influences**
   Covers all the rest of life secrets, some examples are innermost nature of life, source our being, qualities of the soul and spiritual development and divine elements.

Morals are your Karmic responsibility!

Anything can be used for good or bad. Be careful with the power of this information. Many people are extremely vulnerable when they come to an Astrologer who they think can predict their future. They are listening to all your words, and all they will remember is the really good, and especially the really bad information you told them.

What you should _not rely_ on Astrology for:

- Other people's information without their permission (terrible karmic mistake)
- Day to day predictions (it is not fortune telling) Astrology is a guideline; *it will not predict if you are going to be hot by a car today.*

There are many systems used with an astrological chart.

> Even House System, Porphyry House System, and Regiomontanus House System, are to name a few.

This course teaches using the Basic Chart & Even House System

Claudius Ptolemy (100-178) was one of the first astrological writers of the second century. He wrote an astrological book, the Tetrabiblos, which has often been considered the ultimate resource in astrology.

The house system ascribed to Ptolemy through his writings is the Equal house system.

In this method of calculating the house cusps, the degree and minutes of longitude for the Ascendant (the point where the ecliptic intersects the horizon on the eastern side of the meridian) or Midheaven (the point at which the ecliptic and meridian intersect on the south side of the prime vertical) is the starting point.

All the remaining cusps are measured in 30-degree increments from that point.

Thus, each house cusp contains the same degree and minute of longitude as the Ascendant or Midheaven but progresses through the astrological zodiac one sign at a time around the chart wheel.

The Equal house system, therefore, is not "latitude-dependent," and the 4th and 10th house cusps are not on the meridian.

Really what it means is all twelve houses are equal!

The Chart

(birth-chart)

A chart is usually a pictorial graph, which will display all of a person's birth astrology information.

This is the foundation of every type of Astrology. It is essential to have the groundwork prepared before you can build (give any information).

And again, there are many different types and designs of charting.

The two most common in Western Astrology are the; Aries Chart (social chart) and the Natal Chart (personal chart). The only difference is what sign is at the nine o'clock point on the chart or 1st house.

We will be using the Aries chart.

EASTERN ASTROLOGY CHART

Vedic astrology uses a square chart

WESTERN ASTROLOGY CHART

1st STEP: the basis to a western astrology chart is that it is a circle, which is divided into twelve (12) equal pie sections. This circle represents the Earth, and the darker latitude line represents the horizon.

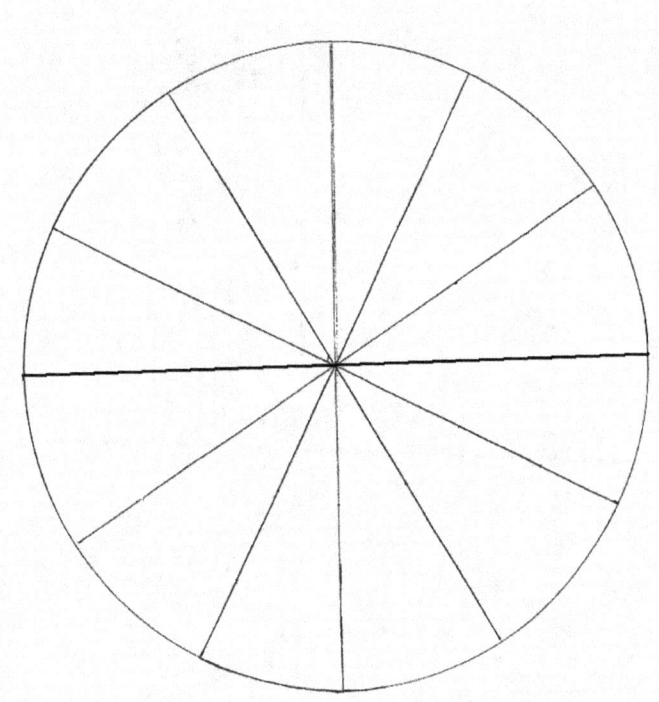

EVEN HOUSE SYSTEM

2nd STEP: the chart is divided into the Even House System.

The houses are always placed in this order, and these locations will never change or move.

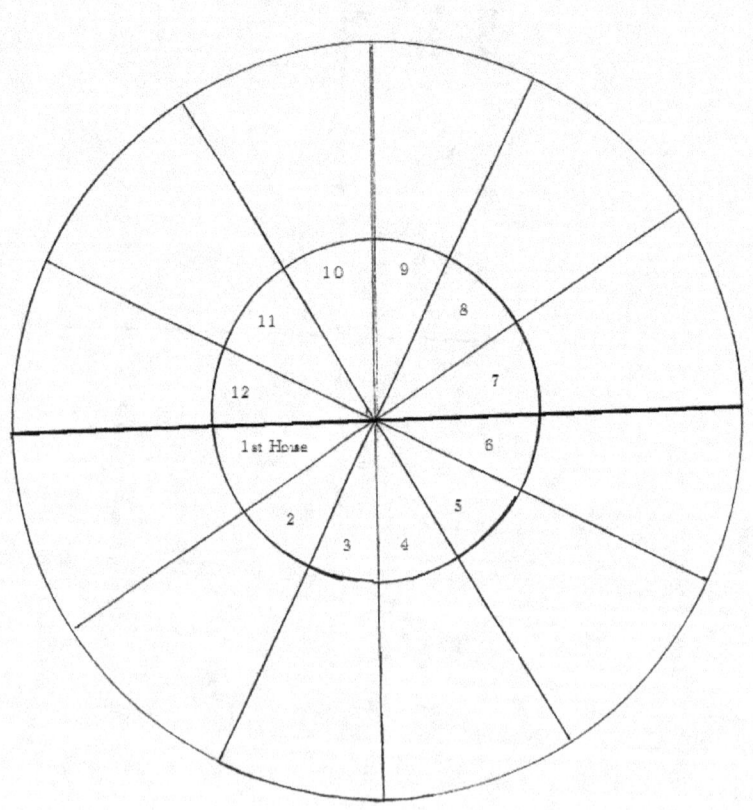

We will discuss the *houses* in more detail in a bit.

ASTROLOGICAL GRAPH REPRESENTATION

3rd STEP: the circle represents the Earth's rotation around the sun in one day (24 hours).

As if you are looking up into the sky (upside down and reversed)

Each house is equal to, 2 hours (12 x 2 = 24).

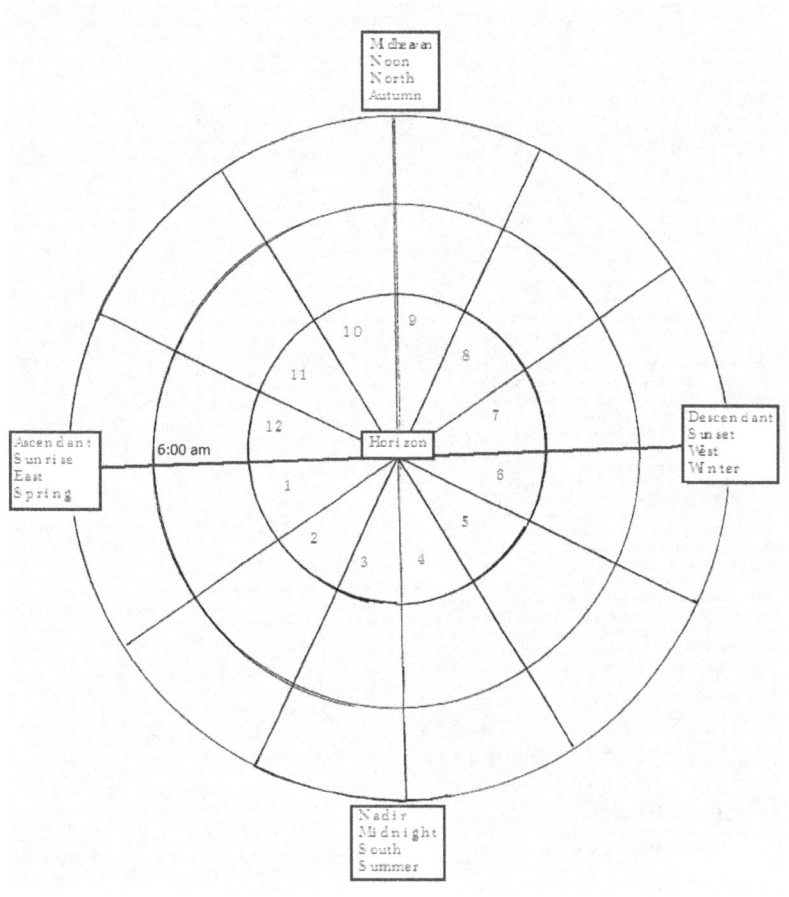

CLOCK - TIME

4th STEP: each section of the pie shape is numbered just like a clock starting at 12 and moving around in the clockwise direction.

A normal house clock goes around twice in one day.

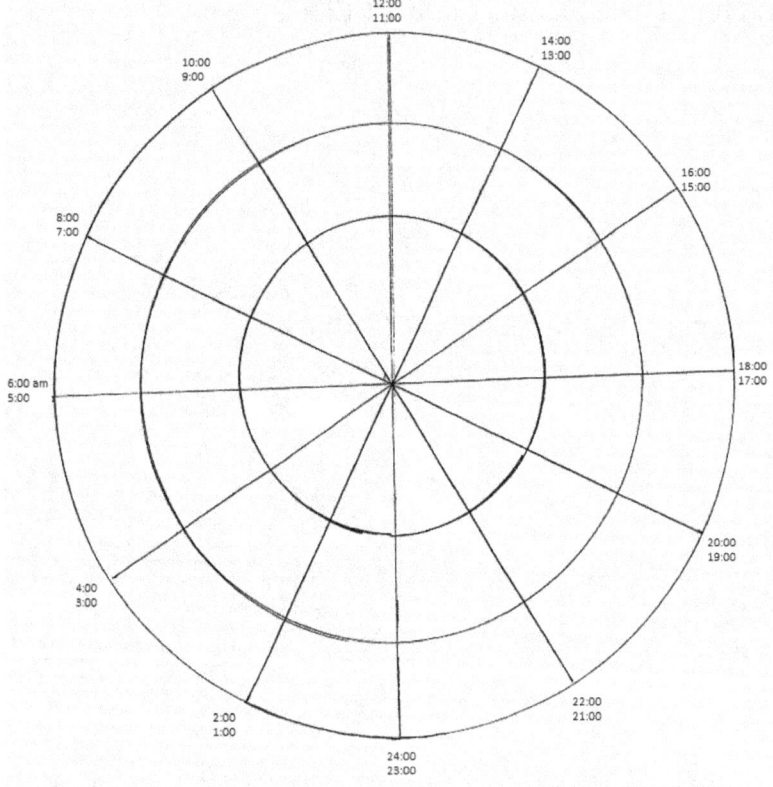

Military Time
1:00 -12:00 hours
13:00 -24:00 hours
Degrees

DEGREES

5th STEP: you will notice each pie shape is 30° (degrees) of the 360° circle.

360° (is a perfect circle) and is equivalent to 1440 minutes (twenty-four hours) in a day
30° is equivalent to 120 minutes (2 hours)
1° is equivalent to 4 minutes

Degrees travel counterclockwise and always start again at one for easy reference in each pie section.

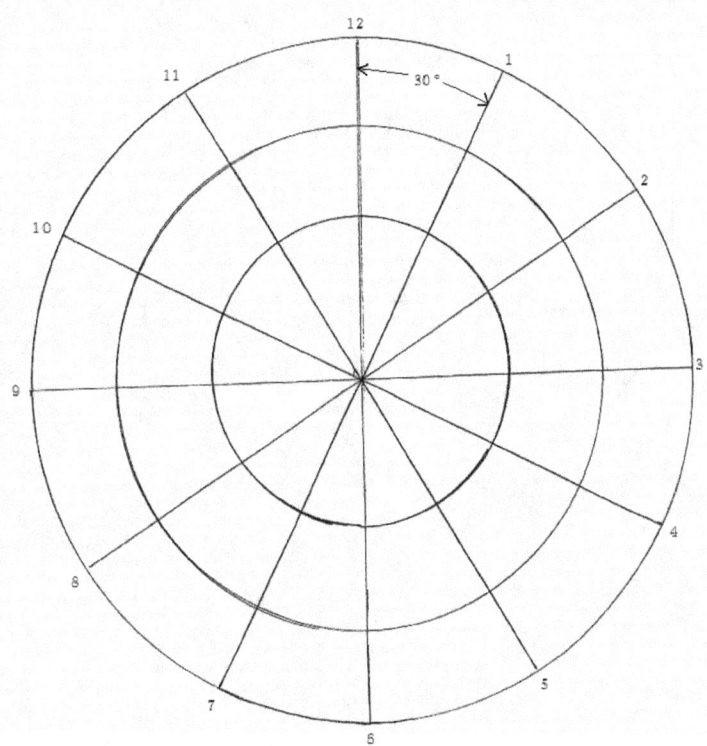

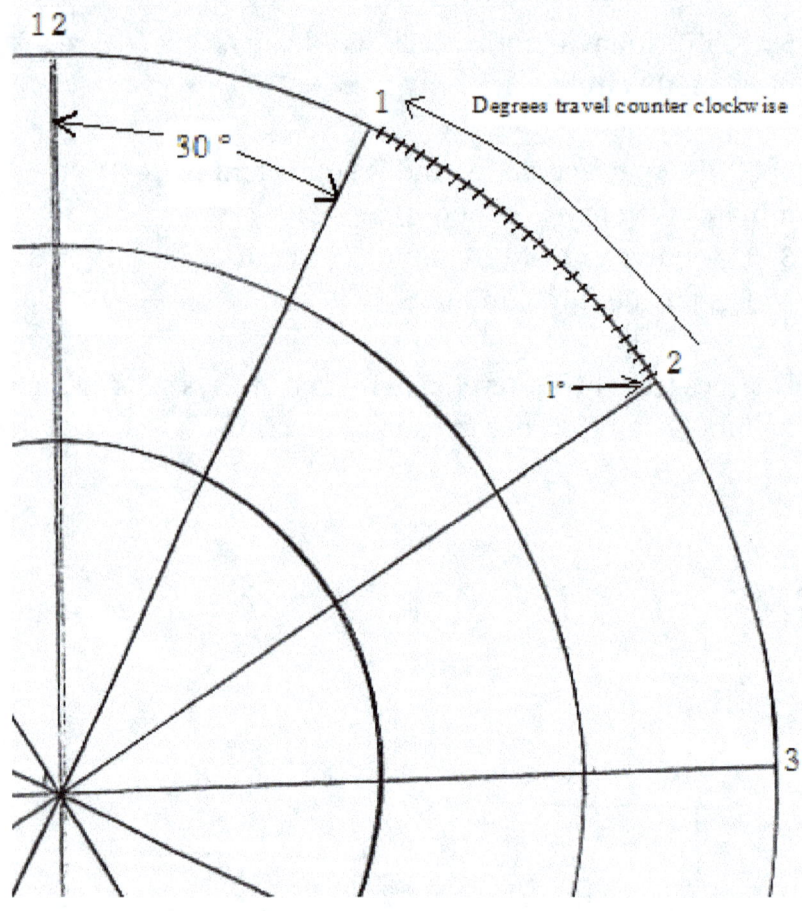

EPHEMERIS

6th STEP: at your birth, the sun, moon, and planets were at an exact spot in the sky. The Ephemeris is a recording of all past and future locations of the sun, moon, and planets.

An ephemeris (plural: ephemerides; from the Greek word ἐφήμερος ephemeros "daily") is a table of values that gives the positions of astronomical objects in the sky at a given time or times. Different kinds are used for astronomy and astrology. Even though this was also one of the first applications of mechanical computers, an ephemeris will still often be a simple printed table.

OCTOBER 2007 — **00:00 UT**

Day	Sid.t	☉	☽	☿	♀	♂	♃	♄	♅	♆	♇	☊	☊	⚸	⚷
M 1	0 37 24	7♎26'24	5♊45	3♏14	24♌45	0♋54	14♐14	3♍26	15°R53	19°R30	26♐27	6°R42	5♓13	8♏29	10°R40
T 2	0 41 21	8°25'23	20° 6	4° 7	25°25	1°21	14°23	3°33	15♓51	19♒29	26°28	6♓39	5°10	8°35	10♒38
W 3	0 45 17	9°24'24	4♋ 4	4°56	26° 6	1°47	14°32	3°39	15°49	19°28	26°28	6°D38	5° 6	8°42	10°37
T 4	0 49 14	10°23'27	17°38	5°43	26°48	2°13	14°41	3°46	15°47	19°27	26°29	6°38	5° 3	8°49	10°36
F 5	0 53 11	11°22'32	0♌51	6°25	27°31	2°38	14°50	3°53	15°45	19°27	26°30	6°39	5° 0	8°56	10°35
S 6	0 57 7	12°21'40	13°44	7° 4	28°15	3° 3	14°59	3°59	15°43	19°26	26°31	6°41	4°57	9° 2	10°34
S 7	1 1 4	13°20'50	26°20	7°38	29° 0	3°28	15° 9	4° 6	15°41	19°25	26°32	6°42	4°54	9° 9	10°33
M 8	1 5 0	14°20'02	8♍44	8° 7	29°47	3°52	15°18	4°12	15°39	19°24	26°33	6°R43	4°51	9°16	10°32
T 9	1 8 57	15°19'17	20°57	8°31	0♍34	4°16	15°28	4°19	15°37	19°23	26°34	6°41	4°47	9°22	10°32
W10	1 12 53	16°18'33	3♎ 2	8°48	1°22	4°39	15°37	4°25	15°35	19°23	26°35	6°38	4°44	9°29	10°31
T 11	1 16 50	17°17'52	15° 1	9° 0	2°10	5° 2	15°47	4°31	15°33	19°22	26°36	6°33	4°41	9°36	10°30
F 12	1 20 46	18°17'13	26°55	9°R 5	3° 0	5°25	15°57	4°38	15°31	19°21	26°37	6°27	4°38	9°43	10°30
S 13	1 24 43	19°16'36	8♏47	9° 2	3°50	5°47	16° 7	4°44	15°29	19°21	26°38	6°18	4°35	9°49	10°29
S 14	1 28 40	20°16'00	20°38	8°52	4°41	6° 8	16°18	4°50	15°27	19°20	26°39	6°10	4°32	9°56	10°29
M15	1 32 36	21°15'27	2♐29	8°34	5°33	6°29	16°28	4°56	15°25	19°20	26°40	6° 1	4°28	10° 3	10°28
T 16	1 36 33	22°14'56	14°24	8° 7	6°26	6°50	16°38	5° 2	15°24	19°19	26°41	5°54	4°25	10° 9	10°28
W17	1 40 29	23°14'26	26°26	7°32	7°19	7°10	16°49	5° 8	15°22	19°19	26°43	5°49	4°22	10°16	10°28
T 18	1 44 26	24°13'59	8♑38	6°48	8°13	7°30	16°59	5°14	15°20	19°18	26°44	5°45	4°19	10°23	10°28
F 19	1 48 22	25°13'33	21° 5	5°56	9° 7	7°49	17°10	5°20	15°18	19°18	26°45	5°D44	4°16	10°29	10°28
S 20	1 52 19	26°13'08	3♒50	4°57	10° 2	8° 7	17°21	5°25	15°17	19°17	26°46	5°44	4°12	10°36	10°D28
S 21	1 56 15	27°12'46	16°58	3°52	10°58	8°25	17°31	5°31	15°15	19°17	26°48	5°45	4° 9	10°43	10°28
M22	2 0 12	28°12'25	0♓33	2°41	11°54	8°43	17°42	5°37	15°14	19°17	26°49	5°R46	4° 6	10°50	10°28
T 23	2 4 9	29°12'06	14°37	1°27	12°51	9° 0	17°53	5°42	15°12	19°16	26°50	5°46	4° 3	10°56	10°28
W24	2 8 5	0♏11'48	29° 8	0°11	13°49	9°16	18° 5	5°48	15°11	19°16	26°52	5°43	4° 0	11° 3	10°28
T 25	2 12 2	1°11'33	14♈ 4	28♎57	14°46	9°32	18°16	5°53	15° 9	19°16	26°53	5°39	3°57	11°10	10°29
F 26	2 15 58	2°11'19	29°17	27°45	15°45	9°47	18°27	5°59	15° 8	19°15	26°55	5°32	3°53	11°16	10°29
S 27	2 19 55	3°11'07	14♉37	26°39	16°44	10° 2	18°38	6° 4	15° 6	19°15	26°56	5°24	3°50	11°23	10°29
S 28	2 23 51	4°10'58	29°53	25°41	17°43	10°15	18°50	6° 9	15° 5	19°15	26°58	5°15	3°47	11°30	10°30
M29	2 27 48	5°10'50	14♊53	24°51	18°43	10°29	19° 1	6°14	15° 4	19°15	26°59	5° 6	3°44	11°37	10°31
T 30	2 31 44	6°10'45	29°30	24°12	19°43	10°42	19°13	6°19	15° 2	19°15	27° 1	4°59	3°41	11°43	10°31
W31	2 35 41	7♏10'42	13♋39	23♎43	20♍44	10♋54	19♐25	6♍24	15♓ 1	19♒15	27♐ 2	4♓54	3♓37	11♏50	10♒32

Delta T = 67.98 sec.

created from Swiss Ephemeris, Copyright Astrodienst AG [5.1.2003]

The placement of sun, moon, and planets are the key information of your personality and the sun, moon, and planets all have a personality of their own.

To figure out your sign placement on the chart, you will need to know; your day, month, and year of your birth, and for an even more accurate reading, the time of your birth is great to have.

*Every chart starts by looking up the information in the Ephemeris.

On the internet, lookup:

- Swiss Ephemeris for the year of ..?.. (Whatever year you are looking for).
- Scroll down to the correct month.

How to read an Ephemeris:

- Go to your Month and Year in the book (make sure you have both books; 1900-2000 & 2000 to 2050)
- Columns
  (Depending on the book or website you are looking in, not necessarily in this order)

  1. Is the day of your birth (date and day of week)
  2. Sid time (Eastern Astrology info - ignore this column).
  3. The Sidereal zodiac is a physical reality depicting commonly acknowledged pictures of groups of stars used by astronomers, Vedic, and Sidereal astrologers.
  4. Most Westerns use the Tropical zodiac is a mathematical construct used by astrologers only.
  5. Sun ☉
  6. Moon ☾
  7. Planet- Mercury ☿
  8. Venus ♀
  9. Mars ♂
  10. Jupiter ♃
  11. Saturn ♄
  12. Uranus ♅
  13. Neptune ♆
  14. Pluto ♇ or P (PL)

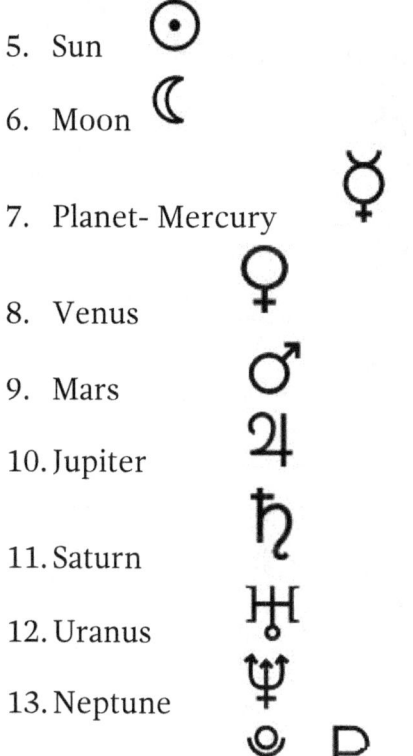

15. Lunar node - Ascending node /north node/Rahu ☊
16. Lunar node - Descending node / south node / Ketu ☋ or ☫
17. The lunar nodes, north, and south, are not real planets. Lunar nodes are points that mark the intersection of the Moon's orbit around the Earth with the ecliptic path. Rahu /Ketu are the personal eclipse points. Therefore, they are areas where you need to work out your Karma, past as well as future. They are our Karmic responsibilities. The nodes always serve opposing purposes- good and bad, lots and nothing, give and take. Rahu gives, Ketu takes back.
18. Asteroid - Pallas / Lilith ⚴ or ⚸
19. Asteroid - Chiron ⚷

ZODIAC SIGNS

7th STEP: In an Aries chart, the signs are always in this order starting at 9 o'clock:

<u>Horoscope Sign</u>

Aries	♈
Taurus	♉
Gemini	♊
Cancer	♋
Leo	♌
Virgo	♍
Libra	♎
Scorpio	♏
Sagittarius	♐
Capricorn	♑
Aquarius	♒
Pisces	♓

We will discuss these more in a bit.

Basic Chart / Aries Chart

This is only an example of a person whose sun sign is in Aries (meaning they were born at the time of day and year when Aries was on the horizon at 6:00 am in the morning).

The zodiac/horoscope signs are placed in this order but will rotate (natal chart) later to show your sign at the horizon (positioned at 9 o'clock, 1st house).

The Aries chart is easy to use as a starting point for all of us to plot our planets at our time of birth.

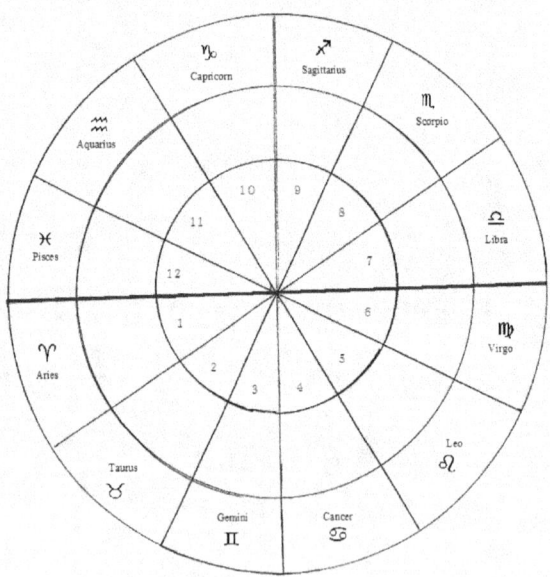

The most important information (core) on any person's chart is where their sun, moon, and ascendant are located. Once a person is born, these three <u>never</u> change.

SUN SIGN ☉ YOUR SOUL

It is determined where the sun was in the sky at the time of your birth.

- Go straight over from your birth date to the third column to find your sun information to put on the graph. (A person born on October 21, 2007 would have the sun sign placement of 27°12'46) this will tell you what horoscope sign you are. Just above your birth date in the Ephemeris is a symbol ♎ to show you what house you are born in.
- The sun sign represents your reputation as if you were in the spotlight, and all eyes were on you. What other people see your personality as?
- What you look up on your horoscope information (though you should read all three to get a true reading, especially in the newspaper)

Example: Oct 21 is in the Libra House ♎

The sun sign ☉ would be placed at 27°12'46 in the Libra house section.

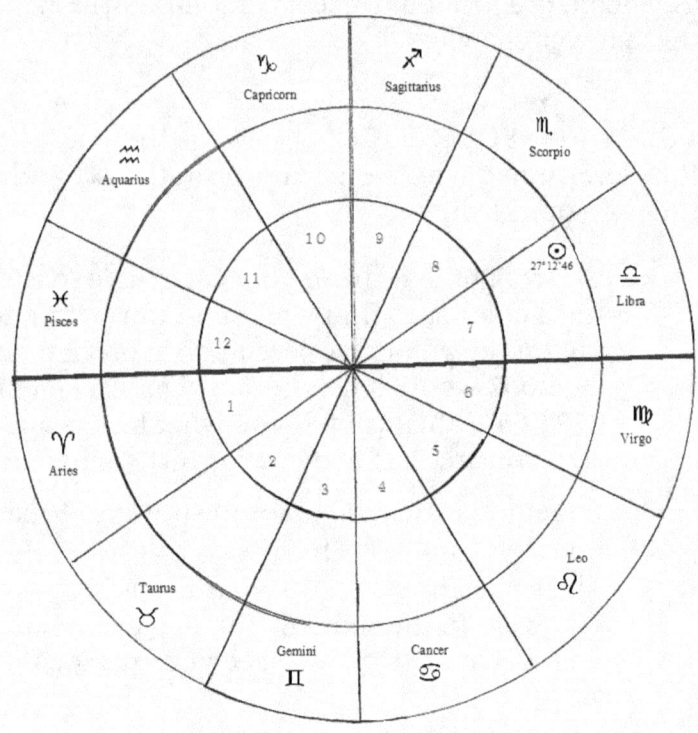

Sun-sign astrology is the form of astrology most commonly found in many newspaper and magazine columns. It is a simplified system of astrology which considers only the position of the Sun, which is said to be placed within one of the twelve zodiac signs depending on the month of birth. This sign is then called the sun sign or star sign of the person born that month.

MOON SIGN ☾ YOUR MIND

It is determined where the moon was in the sky at the time of your birth.

- Go straight over from your birth date to the fourth column to find your moon information to put on the graph. (A person born on October 21, 2007 would have the moon sign placement of 16°58) this will tell you what horoscope sign your moon is in.
- The moon sign influences the type of person you carry yourself as emotionally. How you deal with your emotions.

Example: Oct 21 is in the Capricorn House ♑

The moon sign ☾ would be placed at 16°58 in the Capricorn house section

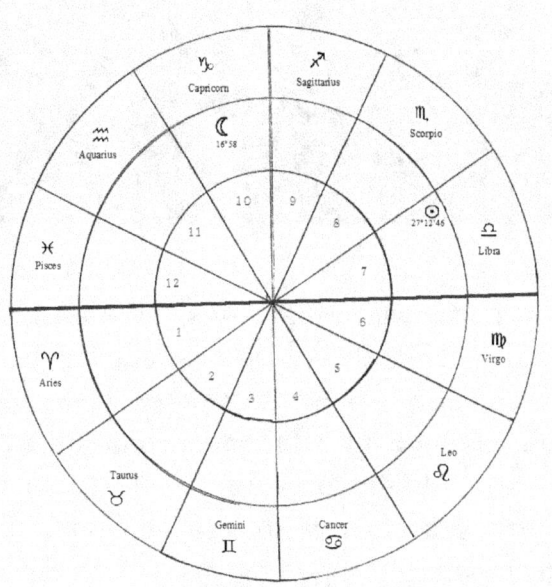

Phases of the Moon

The moon rises in the east and sets in the west. The rising and setting of all celestial objects are due to Earth's continuous daily spin beneath the sky. The moon rises around sunset when it is a full moon, and sunrise when it is a new moon. When you see a thin crescent moon in the west after sunset – it is not a rising moon. Instead, it is a setting moon. The moon moves – with respect to the fixed stars – by about 12 to 13 degrees each day. And on average the moon orbits our Earth every 29.5-days.

Most calendars display the appropriate day of the month for the main moon (lunar) phases. The phases of the moon are determined by the distance between the sun and the moon and the light visible on the moon from Earth. Each phase occurs roughly 7.4 days apart.

A lunar cycle (New Moon to New Moon) is also called a "lunation". During this time, the moon will completely circle the Earth. That is the scientific definition, but you can take any phase; for instance, a so-called "full moon cycle" would be from Full Moon to Full Moon.

MOON PHASES

New Moon

The new moon occurs when the sun and moon are in conjunction, occupying the same part of the sky from the viewpoint of Earth (on the same side of the Earth). During this time, the moon doesn't reflect the light of the sun, and so cannot be seen (except during a solar eclipse). The moon's un-illuminated side is facing the Earth, creating an illusion of a dark moon.

Spiritual meaning (New Beginnings)
The new moon phase is the time of new beginnings - like the Maiden form of the Goddess and the season of Spring. The appearance of the new crescent moon was celebrated as a return of the moon from the dead. This is a time of growing energy, newness, rejuvenation, growth, renewal, and hope. It is a good point to make changes in your life, such as ending bad habits or relationships.

Waxing Crescent

The moon is growing larger in the sky, moving from a narrow crescent just after the new moon towards the full moon. The waxing moon grows from right to left and is called the 'right-hand moon' - the crescent is like the curve between the right-hand's index finger and thumb.

Spiritual meaning (Setting Intentions)
This is the time to set wishes, wants, dreams, desires, and intentions. Create your bucket list. Write out, if you have not already, at least 100 goals to achieve before death.

First Quarter Moon
The moon reaches the first quarter a week after the new moon.

Spiritual meaning (Action)
Once you have set your goals, this is the time of the month to act. Each action you do draws the attention of Spirit, telling them that you are serious about your intention.

Waxing Gibbous
During the phases between the First Quarter and the full moon, and between the full moon and the Last Quarter, when more than half of the disc is illuminated.

Spiritual meaning (Refine)
As you set out to create and manifest your wishes, wants, and desires, you may need to adjust, refine, and shift your actions. This is the best time of the month to do that.

Full Moon
The full moon occurs between 14 and 15 days after the new moon and is shaped like a complete disc. The moon's illuminated side is facing the Earth. The full moon reflects the maximum light from the sun. Meaning the sun and the moon are on opposite sides of the Earth.

Spiritual meaning (Harvest)
This moon phase is the time of abundance, ripening, and completeness - fertile and shining with the full power of feminine secrets and mysteries. This is the time when the moon's energy is strongest and full of magic power.

Be open to receiving your gifts. You have asked, Spirit listened, now prepare yourself to receive.

*If you were born during a time of a full moon, you will feel lunatic during a new moon and vice versa.

Waning Gibbous

The moon is decreasing in size, moving from the full moon back towards a crescent as the new moon approaches. The waning moon decreases from right to left and is called the 'left-hand moon' because of its similarity to the curve on the left hand.

Spiritual meaning (Grateful)
Best time for manifestation. You should be feeling the benefits of your actions. You should see some positive outcomes for your actions.

Last Quarter

As it is making its way back to another new moon, the last quarter moon is the reverse process of the first quarter.

Spiritual meaning (Release)
This is the time that you start to decide if what you manifested was good or bad. We can want something, and after we get it, decide that it was not what we expected. This is the time of the month to reevaluate, release, let go, and forgive.

Waning Crescent

The fraction of the moon that is illuminated is decreasing on its way to becoming a new moon.
Spiritual meaning (Surrender)

You were born with a life purpose, and you will experience your life lessons, so sit back and relax, surrender yourself to the universe. Shift happens... let your months' worth of efforts solidify. If you go, go, go, and do not take a moment to breathe, your intentions will never have enough time to grow. Some things will always be out of your control, and fate must take its course.

We cannot change our past, but each and every day, we have a chance to change our future. You reap what you sow!

Moon months

Our months are linked to the movements of the moon. The moon passes between the Earth and the sun every 29½ days - then there is a new moon. On the Jewish and Muslim calendars, a new month begins, and all the months have 29 or 30 days.

Honey Moon

The June full moon was called the Mead or Honey moon. The name derives from the hives being full of honey at this time of the year. The honey would have been fermented and made into mead. Traditionally, a honey drink was taken after wedding ceremonies held on the Summer Solstice. This is the derivation of 'honeymoon."

Blue Moon

Due to the moon's cycle being 29½ days, there are occasionally - as in July 2004 - two full moons in one month (only happens on average every 2.7 years). Then the second moon of the month is called a 'blue moon'. There will be two blue moons in the year Aug 31, 2012

Dark Moon

When two new moons occur in a month, the second is called a 'dark moon'. The new moon is also sometimes called the dark moon - at this phase, there is no illumination on the Earth's side.

Harvest Moon

The full moon nearest to the Autumn Equinox is called the 'Harvest moon." This is because, for several nights, it appears large and bright in the early evening, bringing farmers valuable extra time to gather in their harvest. The Celtic year was once divided into 13 months - one for each moon occurring during the year.

Lunar eclipse

A lunar eclipse occurs when the Earth passes between the Moon and the Sun. Because full Moons occur when the

Sun and Moon are on opposite sides of the Earth - Lunar eclipses can only happen when the Moon is full. Though not as thrilling as a solar eclipse, the Moon can be seen to magically change color, becoming coppery or even red - this is due to light being reflected from the Earth onto the Moon's surface (known as 'Earthshine'). During the eclipse, you can see the Earth's shadow slowly reach across the surface of the moon.

Moon Void of Course

As the moon orbits the Earth, it passes through the signs of the zodiac (all houses). When the moon is near the end of each sign, it goes beyond its last major aspect or connection with another planet. When this happens, and until it moves into the next sign, the moon is said to be 'Void of Course.'

> This is a time, when you can really feel unconnected and without direction. It is an ideal time though for centering yourself. This condition or feeling may occur for minutes to a couple of days, depending on the location of the planets.
>
> Bad for:
>
> - Avoid making important decisions during this phase of the month
> - Purchases may seem to be unsatisfactory
> - Decisions seem to be unrealistic
> - False starts on new paths
> - Contracts and promises may be more difficult
> - Delays and frustration seem to occur

While the moon is in the couple days of 'Void of Course,' it also takes on the negative traits of that planet it is going through.

Good for:

- Relaxation
- Introspection
- Putting off decisions
- Yoga
- Play
- Sleep
- Meditation

Moon phase is also great to plant a crop by:

- Water signs are most fertile for planting. Irrigate when the moon is in a water sign.
- Fire and Air signs are dry and barren
- Earth signs are moist and productive
- The waxing moon favors the growth of any kind; physical or psychological
- The waning moon favors reduction in growth or size of anything (magnetic pull of the Earth, which pulls energy away from the Earth at New Moon and concentrates energy towards the Earth at the Full Moon.
- You can retard the growth of your lawn by cutting it during a Waning moon and even more when it is in a dry and barren sign.
- Prune trees during the decreasing moon (full to new moon cycle).
- Retard branch growth and make better fruit at the third quarter of Scorpio.
- Cut wood during decreasing moon and <u>not</u> in a water sign.

- Fertilizing is best done in a water sign.
- After Full Moon stimulates root growth, good time to transplant. Seedlings are best transplanted currently and for up to seven days after.
- Three days before a New Moon is the resting time for all plants. Great time for weeding.
- Moon info is used in the Farmer's Almanac Book

ASCENDANT ASC - YOUR PHYSICAL BODY
This is determined from your sun calculations.

- The ascendant sign *ASC* represents your true character. Who you really are?
- Need your time of birth (if you do not know use 12:00 pm/noon)

Example: Oct 21 is in the Libra House ♎

The sun sign ☉ would be placed at 27°12'46 in the Libra house and let's say they were born at 12:43 pm

The formula is:

- Time born   (military time)
    12:43
- calculated into minutes (12 hr x 60 + 43 min)
    763
- divided by 4 (4min =1°)
    763 / 4 = 190.75
- Equals degree
    191°

Start the 191° from your sun sign 27° to get your ascendant *ASC*. (Remember each section of the pie is 30°)

Oct 21 born at 12:43 pm would be 19° in the house of Aries

27° +3° = 30° (finishing ° in Libra)   3
+180° (6x30)   (five more houses)   +180
                                           =183
+8° remaining to get 191°   +8
                                          = 191

Example: Aries Chart Oct 21, 2007 at 12:43 pm = Asc 8° Taurus

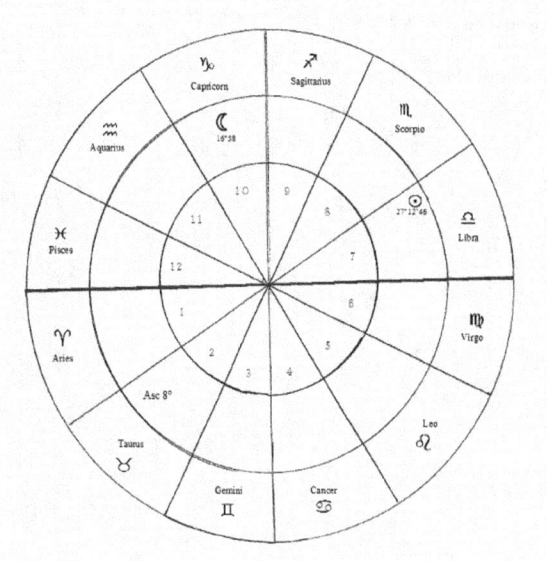

This person born Oct 21 at 12:43 would have a Taurus 8° ascendant (ASC)

With the Sun, Moon and Ascendant marked on the chart

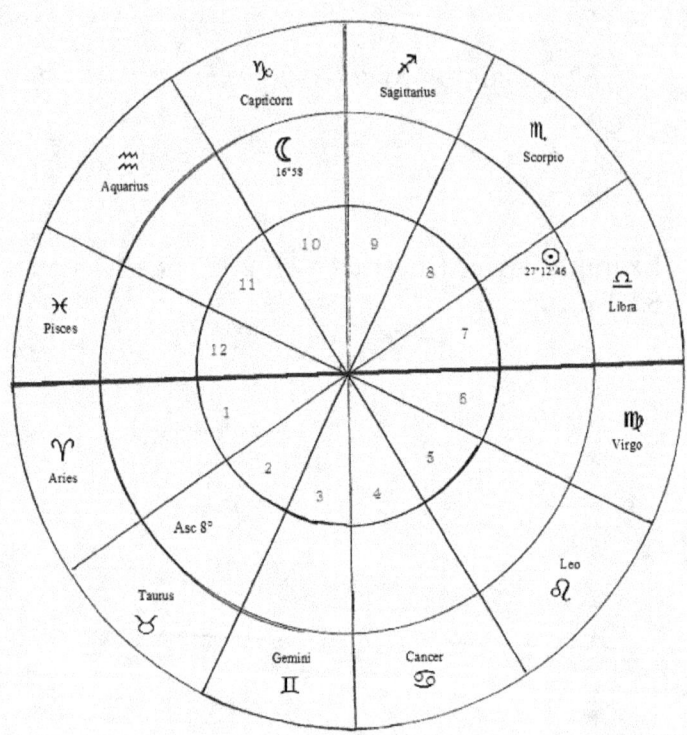

The difference with a **Natal Chart** is the ascendant, sun & moon move houses. Taurus 8° is placed in the 1st house at 6:00am, the moon is in the 9th house, and the sun is in the 6th house.

Overview of the Core planets:

- Sun Sign/Zodiac sign — How others see you
- Moon Sign — Emotions
- Ascendant — How you really are

Homework:

1. Find your House month using the Western dates
2. Look up your Sun sign in the Ephemeris

Make a copy of the chart in the back of the manual:

3. Place the Sun sign and the degrees in the correct placement on your Aries chart (remember the house is divided into 30° place to your information)
4. Place the Moon sign and the degrees in the correct placement on your Aries chart
5. Place the Ascendant and the degrees in the correct placement on your Aries chart
6. Write out the basic meaning of the three

HOUSES
Areas of Life Expression

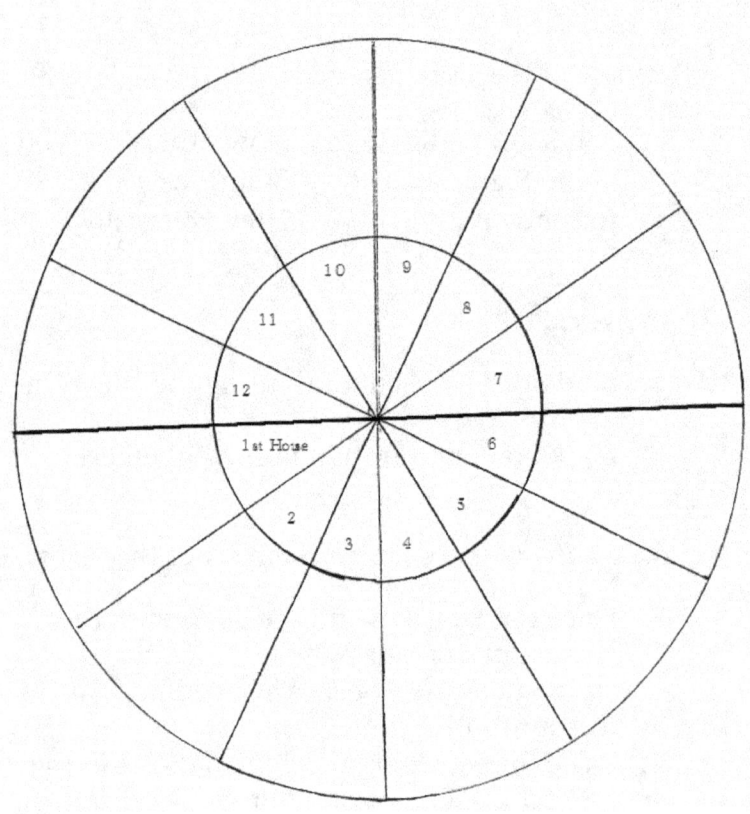

Houses of Life	**1, 5, 9**
Houses of Wealth	**2, 6, 10**
Houses of Relationships	**3, 7, 11**
Houses of Endings	**4, 8, 12**

The 1-6 houses represent your inner world (all about me)

1st House represents: Body

- Beginnings
- Who you are / personality / ego
- Physical appearance
- Psychological motivation / what makes you go

2nd House: Finances

- Wealth matters
- Possessions
- Physical items you can pick up and move
- Materialistic

3rd House: Siblings

- Communication – verbal
- Expression
- Memory / mind / logic
- Relatives, brothers, sisters

4th House: Happiness & Comforts

- Home
- Domestic life
- Security
- Parents (mother & father) if you are living at home
- Your upbringing

5th House: Children

- Self-expression
- Creativity
- Love & romance
- Children
- Amusement & fun

6th House: Enemies

- Health / diet
- Constitution
- Service / Community interaction

These 7-12 houses represent your outer world (how you are in the world)

7th House: Wife

- Partnership & Relationships (marriage)
- Social interaction
- How do I interact in society
- Feel & relate

8th House: Death

- Secrets / what you hide / skeletons in the closet
- Life; birth & death
- Intimacy / sex
- Change

9th House: Fortune

- Travel
- Education
- Legalities
- Writing / physically doing it
- Communication / philosophy

10th House: Occupation

- Career / work / ambition
- What you do to afford your possessions
- Responsibility
- Authority

11th House: Gain & Profits

- Friendship
- Hopes / Dreams / Wishes
- Dreamer / new experiences
- Freedom / humanitarian activities

12th House: Expenditures & Loss

- Closure / endings / completion
- Spiritual involvement
- Subconscious
- Sorrows

QUADRANTS
Viewed as if you are looking up into the night`s sky.

The astrology chart is also divided into 4 quadrants: North, South, East, and West

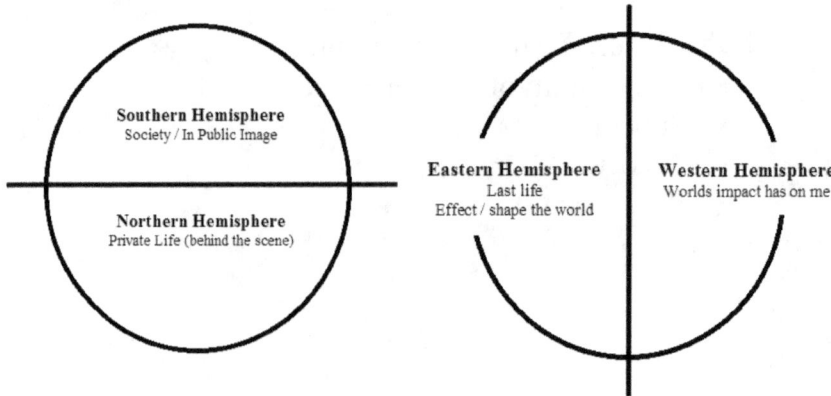

Depending on where the majority of planets are.

Southern Hemisphere - Social & Public life

- Outer aim
- People oriented
- Career / professional life
- Involved with community / world at large
- Public approval gives them satisfaction
- Like to be seen

Northern Hemisphere - Emphasis on self and family

- Inner aim
- Private life
- Do not like to be in the limelight

- Personal pursuits and pleasures
- Inner goals and satisfaction
- Like to be hidden

Eastern Hemisphere - Person's impact on the world

- Shape / mold the world
- Thinking kind of person
- Past life Karma

Western Hemisphere - World's impact on the person

- Shaped / molded by circumstance
- Doing kind of person
- Portray

Four Quarters

Need four or more planets in a quarter

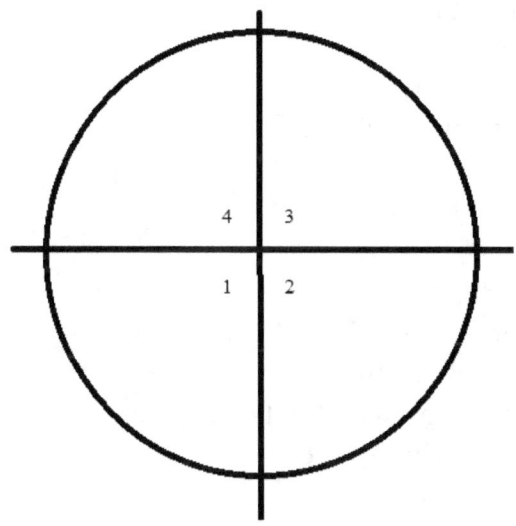

1st

- Highly assertive individuals
- Strong personalities
- Self-assertive and motivated
- Develop young to make their mark
- Not high staying power to get things done
- Pushy people

2nd

- Relationship oriented
- Need companionship for motivation
- Need to know someone is there
- Work with people

3rd

- Outer directed
- Ambitious but need cooperation from others to achieve a goal
- Very adaptable
- Outgoing
- Socially focused
- Need people around

4th

- Most independent
- Most ambitious of all
- Make their own way
- Gain through own efforts
- Depend on themselves
- Self-sufficient

- Will succeed no matter what attitude
- Do not require other people around

Zodiac Signs

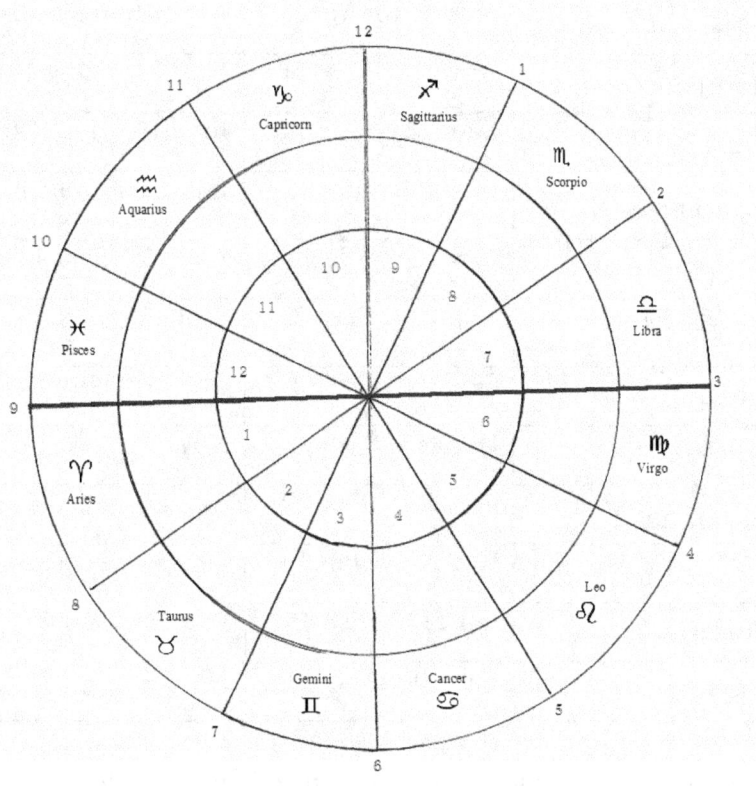

In an Aries chart, the signs are always in this order:

We will use the western dates *(Western dates accuracy is depending on the year you were born, dates are approximate)*

Sign	Western Dates	Eastern Dates (Vedic)
Aries ♈	Mar 21 to Apr 20	April 15 to May 14
Taurus ♉	Apr 21 May 21	May 15 June 14
Gemini ♊	May 22 June 21	June 15 July 14
Cancer ♋	June 22 July 22	July 15 Aug 14
Leo ♌	July 23 Aug 22	Aug 15 Sept 14
Virgo ♍	Aug 23 Sept 22	Sept 15 Oct 14
Libra ♎	Sept 24 Oct 23	Oct 15 Nov 14
Scorpio ♏	Oct 24 Nov 22	Nov 15 Dec 14
Sagittarius ♐	Nov 23 Dec 22	Dec 15 Jan 14
Capricorn ♑	Dec 23 Jan 20	Jan 15 Feb 14
Aquarius ♒	Jan 21 Feb 19	Feb 15 Mar 14
Pisces ♓	Feb 20 Mar 20	Mar 15 Apr 14

What this is showing you is that your birthdate may be an altogether different horoscope sign in Eastern Astrology. I am born Aug 10, and in the Western chart, I am a Leo, but in the Eastern chart, I am a Cancer.

The *Zodiac Signs* are based on the constellation (Stars in the sky)

The ancients designed the astrological signs starting in the spring equinox, and Aries was the first constellation at the start of the spring equinox.

ZODIAC SIGNS = PERSONALITY

Just as each aspect of the sun, moon, ascendant, and house have personality tendencies, so does your Zodiac sign. The sign that signifies and tells your personality traits that you were born with. As each day of the month is important, so is each day of the year. Each of the twelve moon cycles has been granted a Zodiac sign. Even though the date of each sign is a bit different, in both Eastern and Western astrology, the personality traits and the start of a chart are ALWAYS the same, with Aries.

Why all of these are important is because if I say to someone I live on Earth, they may answer where? If I reply by saying North America, they may answer where? If I say Canada, they may answer where? If I say British Columbia, they may answer where? If I say Kelowna, they may answer where? So, until I say exactly which house I live in, all the facts are not there.

This is what you are doing on the horoscope chart; you are fine-tuning the facts.

Aries ♈ *Ram*

March 21 to April 20

Ruled by the planet Mars

- Energetic
- On the go
- Boarder-line work alcoholics
- Gets bored very fast
- Frustrated if nothing gets done
- Can motivate others by example
- Does not like to follow rules
- Passion is their driving force
- No patience
- Want things yesterday
- Temper tantrums, 2-year olds of the signs

Taurus ♉ *Bull*

April 21 to May 21

Ruled by the planet Venus Earth

- Ability to work within the limits of the surrounding
- Doesn't move
- Very patient
- He who has the most toys wins
- How much do you own
- Not about the dollar or looks, does it do the job!
- <u>Major</u> stubborn
- Great to follow rules, if they agree to them
- Do not forget
- They will get it, may take longer but they will succeed
- Strongest constitution (health)
- Never know when they are going to snap

INTUITIVE LIFE – GIFT OF PROPHECY | 193

Gemini ♊ *Twins*

May 22 to June 21

Ruled by the planet Mercury

- Fun
- Can multitask very well
- They live for communication
- Need to be heard
- Will argue both sides of any argument
- Need to make a point
- Pick four directions and try to go in all four
- Cannot make decisions well or fast
- Do not like to have many choices
- Need very clear precise directions

Cancer ♋ *Crab*

June 22 to July 22

Ruled by the Moon ☾   Cruithne

- All about house and home
- Home based
- Caretaker
- Betty Crocker / homemaker
- Appear cold, hard, and detached (not true)
- Born with a wall up
- Inside soft and mushy
- Emotional
- Tend to run off instinct
- Drawn to occult information

Leo ♌ *Lion*

July 23 to August 22

Ruled by the Sun ☉   Vulcan

- Either very energetic or very lazy
- Don't always follow the rules
- If everything is going good, they will ignore it
- If ever ticked off, watch out
- Do not push them too far
- They will scream (roar) before they bit
- Very creative / artistic
- Entertainers
- Their mind catches (imagines) the weirdest things

Virgo ♍ *Virgin*

August 23 to September 22

Ruled by the planet Mercury ☿ Chiron ⚷

- Healer / Dr. / Psychiatrist
- Picky
- Extreme attention to perfection
- Can tell if anything is wrong
- Looking out for the individual (helper)
- Everything must be in order
- Do not like change

Libra ♎ *Scale*

September 24 to October 23

Ruled by the planet Venus ♀

- Need balance
- Debutants
- Fashion-conscious
- Love lots of company
- Spotlight
- Egocentric
- I want it all, and I want everyone to know I have it all

Scorpio ♏ *Scorpion*

October 24 to November 22

Ruled by the planet Mars ♂ Pluto ♀

- Information monger
- Usually correct in one or two areas, but will make it up in others
- Good at keeping secrets / hidden information
- Are good at getting a secret out of someone
- Way out there
- Love taboo topics
- Acutely aware of life after death and the cycle of life
- Nymphomaniac
- Strongest interest in the occult of all the signs

Sagittarius ♐ *Archer*

(Half man, half horse - centaur)

November 23 to December 22

Ruled by the planet Jupiter ♃

- Thinkers
- Writers / note takers
- Good at record-keeping
- If they make a mistake, they will fix it
- Legal
- Truth seekers
- Strict facts
- Will do the nitty-gritty jobs
- May be boring at parties
- Narrow-minded
- Lots of energy / passion for what they do
- Disconnected / watcher
- Great investors / finance

Capricorn ♑ *Goat*

December 23 to January 20

Ruled by the planet Saturn

- Taskmaster
- Organizers
- Teachers
- Great bookkeepers
- Mental building / planners
- Stubborn
- Stability
- Martyrs (always their fault)
- Do not like change unless they do it
- Not too picky

Aquarius ♒ *Water-bearer*

January 21 to February 19

Ruled by the planet Saturn ♄   Neptune

- Humanitarians
- Let's all get along
- For the greater good
- Community group gatherings
- Green peace / animal activists
- Tendency to put other people first
- Group hugs
- Stress level very high
- Methods are skewed = ideas are right, short-sided to practicality

Pisces ♓ *Two fish*

February 20 to March 20

Ruled by the planet Jupiter ♃ Uranus

- Extremist
- Happy to angry to happy in seconds
- Manic depressive
- Moody
- Reactionary
- Looks for different ways of doing things
- New way
- Extreme fixers / put it back proper
- Strongest of the occult – most evolved psychic, sensitive
- Do not relate to reality well

Planets

More to add to your collection of facts... To ancient astrologers, the planets represented the will of the gods and their direct influence upon human affairs. To modern astrologers, the planets represent basic drives or impulses in the human psyche.

Sun ☉ or **Vulcan** (usually the sun, but the sun cannot travel around itself)

Leadership

- Tell others what to do
- I am in control

Moon ☽

Emotions

- How do you feel
- Huggers

Mercury ☿

Communication   Not necessarily in person (face to face)

- Equipment
- Verbal
    - Telephone
    - Internet
    - Mail

Venus ♀

Appearances   Notice me

- Looks /fashion
- Trend / fad

Mars ♂

Passion planet   Whatever you love to do

- Drive
- Impulse
- Heart

Jupiter ♃

Expansion / Deduction

- Money / finances / cash flow
- Business growth
- Cycle that grows bigger or smaller

Saturn ♄

Teacher

- Lessons in life (depending on the house it is in)
- Big obstacles / challenges
- Successes

Uranus ⛢

Endings / Beginnings

- End all be all
- Real wisdom
- Heartfelt understanding
- Life goal

Neptune ♆

Trouble inborn conflicts

- Hidden thoughts
- Subconscious drive
- Personality

Pluto ♇ or P (PL)

Draw to secrets

- Hidden information
- They want to know outside the norm
- Birth / Death

Earth 🜨

Possessions

- Material world   Value
- He who has most toys wins

Chiron ⚷

Caretaker

- Nursemaid
- Healer

More expression of personality

Qualities

Cardinal *House 1, 4, 7, 10*

- **Do it my way**
- Starters
- Leaders
- Extra energy / lots of get up and go

Fixed *House 2, 5, 8, 11*

- **It is getting done**
- Stubborn
- Stable / traditional
- Will not change willingly
- Heels dug in / Not going to move

Mutable *House 3, 6, 9, 12*

- **Do not care how, just get it done**
- Adaptable
- Changeable on a dime
- Can see all sides

Elements Personality

Fire *House 1, 5, 9*

- Passion driven
- Doers / starters
- Get bored easy

Earth *House 2, 6, 10*

- Grounded / practical
- Stable
- Workers
- Finishers / get things done

Air *House 3, 7, 11*

- Thinkers / Intellectual
- Communicative
- Inventive
- Co-operative nature

Water *House 4, 8, 12*

- Emotional
- Intuitive
- Compassion
- Artistic

Aspects / Angles:

Angular Houses – Planets in these houses indicate some prominence in the world.

Main
1. <u>Trine</u>
    - 2 planets 120°

2. <u>Grand Trine</u>
    - 3 planets 120°
    - *Most beneficial connection*
3. <u>Conjunction</u>
    - sitting on top
    - 8° variance to one side or other
    - *Two planets will get along and work beautifully together.*
4. <u>Opposition</u>
    1. 180° other side
    2. 6° variance
    3. *If working together, great*
    4. *If fighting –awful*
5. <u>Square</u>
    - 90° angle
    - *If working together great*
    - *If fighting –awful*
6. <u>Sextiles</u> width of 2 houses apart
    - 60°
    - *Very compatible*

7. <u>Nothing</u>
    - No planet in a house
    - *No issue at all*

Aspect - Any ° (degree) of angle

Also mean something but not taught in this course

Order

Degree	Name	ORB	-variance
0	Conjunct	9	0-9
14	Semi-conjunct	4	10-18
20	Seminovile	1	19-21
22.5	1/16	½	22-23
25.71	Semiseptile	1 ½	24-26
30	Semisextile	3	27-33
36	Decile	2	34-38
40	Novile	1	39-41
45	Semisquare	3	42-48
51.42	Septile	1 ½	49-53
60	Sextile	6	54-66
67.5	3/16	½	67-68
72	Quintile	3	69-75
77.13	Semibiseptile	1 ½	76-78
80	Binovile	1	79-81
90	Square	8	82-98
99.5	Semibinovile	½	99-100
102.84	Biseptile	1 ½	101-104
108	Tridecile	3	105-111

112.5	5/16	½	112-113
120	Trine	6	114-126
128.55	Semitriseptile	1 ½	127-129
130.5	Squarenovile	½	130-131
135	Sesquiquadrate	3	132-138
139.5	Binovextile	½	139-140
144	Biquintile	3	141-147
150	Quincunx	2	148-152
154.26	Triseptile	1 ½	153-156
157.5	7/16	½	157-158
160	Quadranovile	1	159-161
166	Semiopposition	4	162-170
180	Opposition	9	171-180

Patterns

b means blank.

These are examples - not necessarily in this order.

Can have more than one pattern, look at dominate one.

Splash

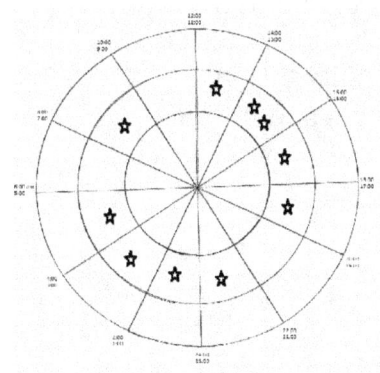

1,2,1   1,b,1   1,1,1
b,1,b

The planets occupy as many signs as possible

- many interests
- studies / reads many topics
- may be proficient in many areas
- may scatter energy

Splay

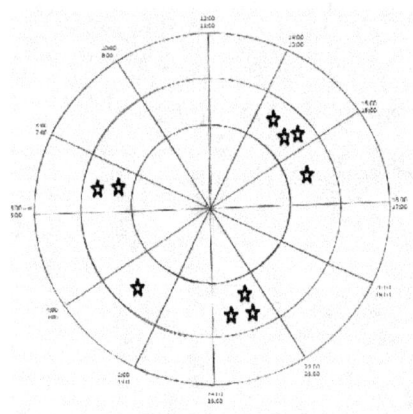

b,b,1   1,b,b   3, b, 1
b,2,b

Similar to splash, but at least one stellium (3 or more planets in one sign)

- Very individual / loners
- Refuses to be regimented by other people's rules or conventions
- Tends to have unusual tastes and interest
- Will follow those dictates and no one else's
- Own rules

Bundle

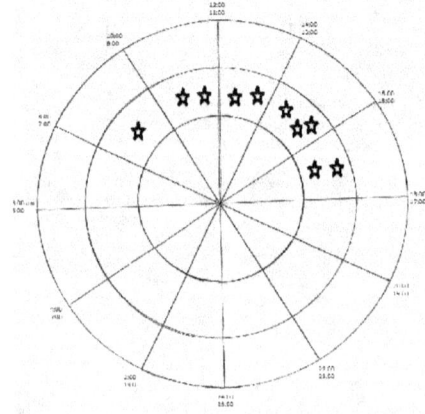

b,b,b   b,b,b   b,1,2,
2,3,2

Planets closely grouped together in very few signs

Signs must all be consecutive. Rarest pattern

- The individual is a specialist
- Work or interest revolves around one concern or one point of view
- Do best applying themselves to one subject and become an expert
- Can be very scientific

Locomotive

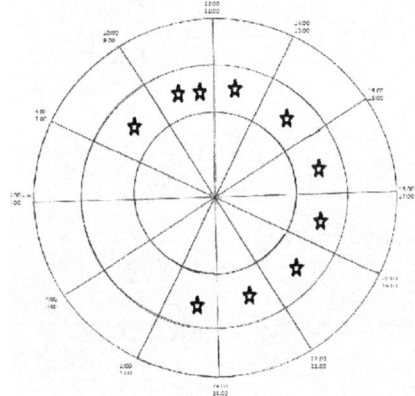

1,2,1   1,1,1 1,1,1
b,b,b

Planets range over a large number of consecutive signs. Like a train

Leading planet in clockwise rotation is the strongest

- Deal with a situation with drive and energy
- Have many resources
- Dominate planet and house
- Usually an indication of what area the person is strong in

Bowl

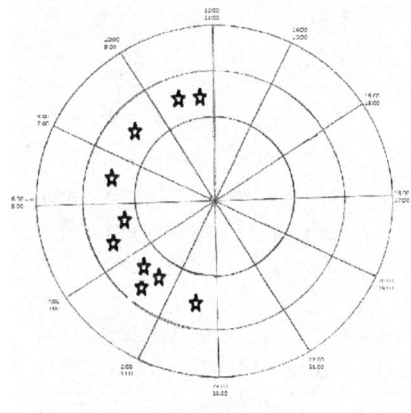

1,1,2   b,b,b b,b,b
1,3,2

All planets fall within six consecutive signs

- Thoughtful & self-contained
- Learn and profit from experiences in life
- Particularly forceful personalities (when all planets are in one hemisphere)

Bucket

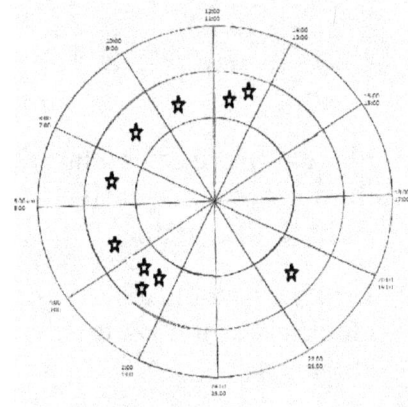

b,1,b   b,3,1   1,1,1
2,b,b

All but one or two planets together form in one hemisphere. Can see where the focus is.

- Single-minded drive
- Marshal their energies in one direction
- Often the singleton (the left-over planets- indicate the goal or direction to pursue)

See-Saw / Bowtie

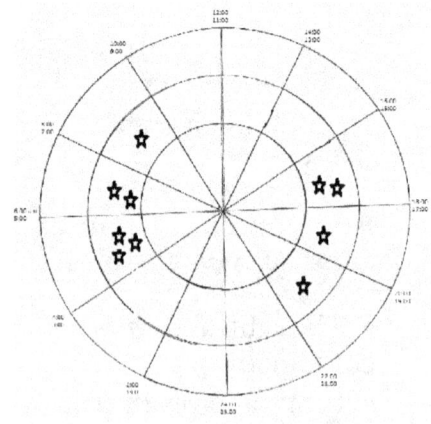

1,b,b   b,3,2   1,b,b,
b,2,1

Roughly placed planets on two sides of the circle with at least two empty signs on either side of the see-saw

- Always see two sides of a situation
- Take into consideration opposing viewpoints and opinions
- Weigh these when making their decision

Astrology Charting Procedure

First, create the chart

- Look up birth; year, date and time in the Ephemeris
- Chart the Sun, Moon, and Ascendant
- Chart all planets
- Rotate chart using the Ascendant point to be at 6:00am horizon
- Check what planets are in which house
- Check quadrants, qualities, elements, angles, and patterns

Second, interpret the chart

Collecting all the facts.

- Tendencies
- Actions
- Planets
- Qualities
- Elements

Remember, a person wants

- To know what Karma you have (what you were born with)
- How they can change their Karma, if possible
    - Confirmation
    - Guidance
    - Direction
    - Options

People are interested in Health, Wealth, and Happiness... *and when their luck is going to change!*

Quick reference:

Tendencies:

Signs =	Personality
Houses =	Areas of Life expression – life, wealth, relationships, endings
Planets =	Basic drives or impulses

Action:

Angels =	Issues / problems / weakness

Planets:

Vulcan /Sun	Leadership
Moon	Emotions
Mercury	Communication
Venus	Appearance / Looks
Mars	Passion / Drive
Jupiter	Money / Finances
Saturn	Teacher / Lessons
Uranus	Endings / Beginnings, life goal
Neptune	Trouble / Conflict
Pluto	Secrets, Birth / Death
Earth/opp sun	Possessions
Chiron	Caretaker / Healer

Qualities:

    Cardinal: *House 1, 4, 7, 10*

        Do it my way, starters, leaders, extra energy (lots of get up and go)

    Fixed: *House 2, 5, 8, 11*

        It's getting done, Stubborn, Stable, traditional, no change, not going to move

    Mutable: *House 3, 6, 9, 12*

        Just get it done, adaptable, changeable on a dime, can see all sides

Elements: Personality

    Fire: *House 1, 5, 9*

        Passion driven, doers/starters, get bored easily

    Earth: *House 2, 6, 10*

        Grounded / practical, stable, workers, finishers (get things done)

    Air: *House 3, 7, 11*

        Thinkers/Intellectual, communicative, inventive, co-operative

    Water: *House 4, 8, 12*

        Emotional, intuitive, compassion, artistic

The average reading is over $100.00, with three pages; Chart and at least a two-page description

People want:

- Confirmation
    o Personal info about themselves (Sun, Moon, Asc...)
- Direction & Guidance
    o How to shift their lives for the better.

These NEVER change,
if it is in House 1, it stays in House 1!!!

House	Sign	Ruled By (Lord)	Qualities	Element	Gender
1	Aries	Mars	Cardinal	Fire	Male
2	Taurus	Venus	Fixed	Earth	Female
3	Gemini	Mercury	Mutable	Air	Male
4	Cancer	Moon	Cardinal	Water	Female
5	Leo	Sun	Fixed	Fire	Male
6	Virgo	Mercury	Mutable	Earth	Female
7	Libra	Venus	Cardinal	Air	Male
8	Scorpio	Mars & Ketu	Fixed	Water	Female
9	Sagittarius	Jupiter	Mutable	Fire	Male
10	Capricorn	Saturn	Cardinal	Earth	Female
11	Aquarius	Saturn & Rahu	Fixed	Air	Male
12	Pisces	Jupiter	Mutable	Water	Female

INTUITIVE LIFE – GIFT OF PROPHECY | 219

Master Horoscope Chart

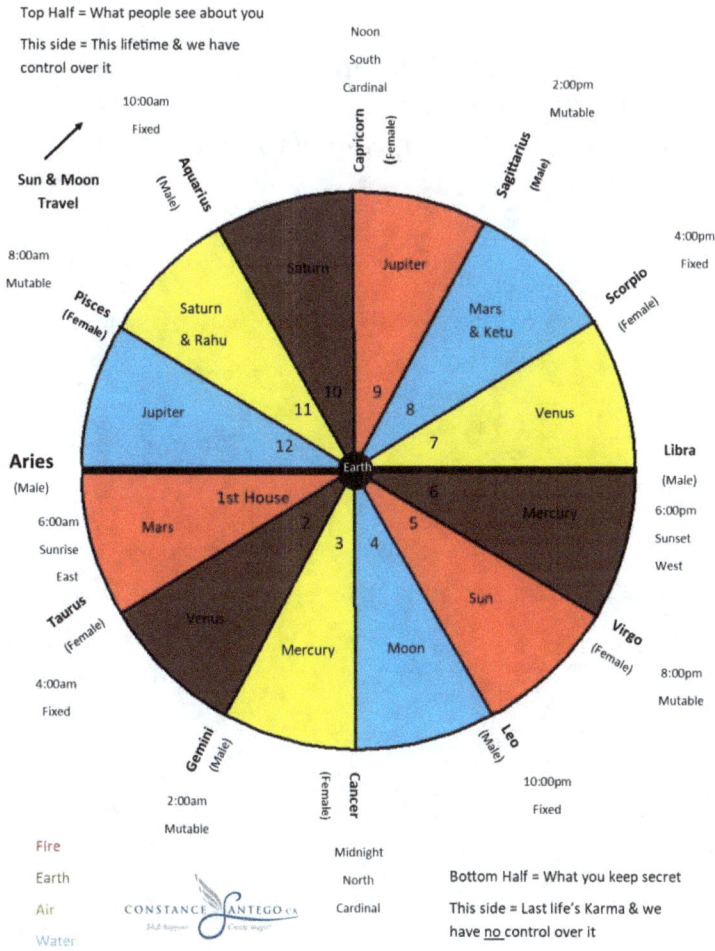

Homework

- Place all the remaining planets form the Ephemeris onto your Aries chart.
- Cut out the middle (Houses) on the chart and turn the Ascendant to 6:00 am and tape in place – Becomes a Natal Chart
- Write out the basic meaning to each planet.

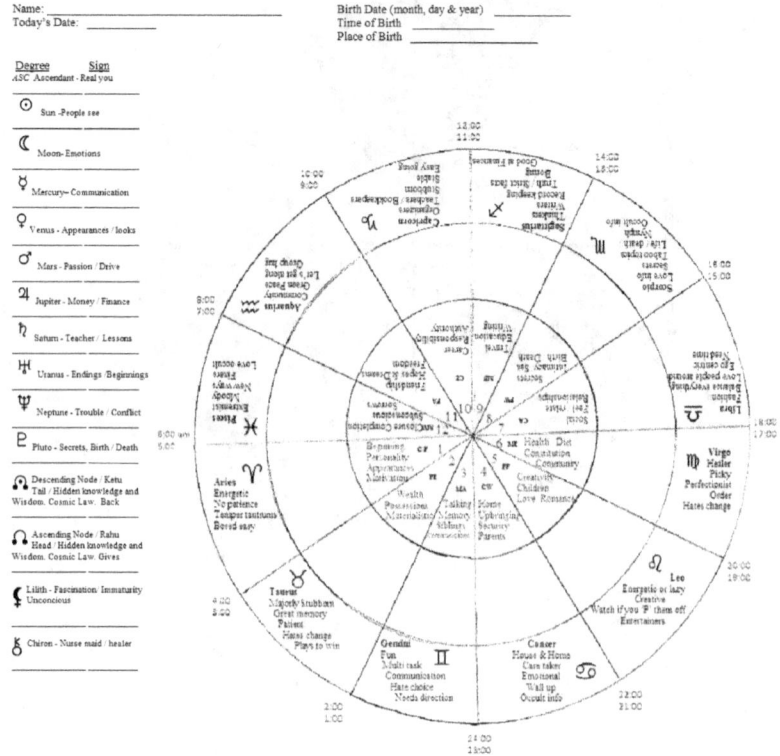

Reader: _____

Basic Meaning

Asc

_____
_____
_____
_____

Sun ☉

_____
_____
_____
_____

Moon ☾

_____
_____
_____
_____

Mercury ☿

_____
_____
_____
_____

Venus ♀

_____
_____
_____
_____

Mars ♂

Jupiter ♃

Saturn ♄

Uranus ⛢

Neptune ♆

Pluto ♇

Ascending node / Rahu ☊

_____
_____
_____
_____

Descending node / Ketu ☋ or ☋

_____
_____
_____
_____

Lilith ⚸

_____
_____
_____
_____

Chiron

_____
_____
_____
_____

Summery

_____
_____
_____
_____
_____
_____
_____
_____

Specific Question (s)

Bibliography - Appendices

Appendix I: A Suggested Reading List

There are many books available to further your learning on the topics covered in this course; those listed here are some suggestions:

Ascended Masters
King, Godfrey Ray
        Unveiled Mysteries (Saint Germain Series; Vol.1).
    1989   The Magic Presence (Saint Germain Series; Vol. 2).

Sandweiss, Samuel H.
    1975   Sai Baba: The Holy Man and the Psychiatrist. San Diego, California: Birth Day Publishing Company

Stone, Joshua David
    1995   Ascended Masters Light the Way. Sedona, Arizona: Light Technology. Publications.

Aura and Psychometry
Brennan, Barbara
    1988   Hands of Light: a Guide to Helaing Through the Human Energy Field. Bantam
        Books.

Butler, W.E.
    1978   How to Read the Aura, Practice Psychometry, Telepathy and Clairvoyance.
        Indiana: Warner Destiny Books

Body Scan
Sugrue, Thomas
    1942   The Story of Edgar Cayce. New York, New York: Dell Publishing Company.

Chakras
Arguelles, Jose
    1987   The Mayan Factor: Path Beyond Technology.

Beinfield, Harriet and Korngold, Efrem
    1991   A Guide to Chinese Medicine. New York: Ballantine Books.

Castaneda, Carlos
    1974   Tales of Power. New York, New York: Pocket Books

Energy Healing
Brennan, Barbara Ann
    1987   Hands of Light. New York, New York: Bantam Books.

Guides
Altea, Rosemary
    1995   The Eagle and the Rose. New York, New York: Warner Books Inc.

Eadie, Betty J.
    1992   Embraced By The Light. New York: Bantam Books.
    1996   The Awakening Heart. New York, New York: Pocket Books.

Guggenheim, Bill
    1995   Hello From Heaven. New York: Bantam Books.

Van Praagh, James
    1997   Talking to Heaven. New York, New York: Penguin Group

Healing
Steiger, Brad
    1971   Kahuna Magic. Westchester, Pennsylvania: Whitford Press.

Gienger, Michael
    2004   Crystal Power, Crystal Healing. London, U.K.: Blandford

Hay, Louise L.
    1988   Heal Your Body. Carlsbad, California: Hay House, Incorporated.

Manifesting
Small Wright, Machaelle
    1983   Behaving As If The God in All Life Mattered. Jefferson, Virginia: Perelandra.

Numerology
Adler, Irving
    1974   Magic House of Numbers. New York, New York: The John Day Company.

Goodman, Morris C.
    1968   Modern Numerology. New York: Paperback Library.

Pendulums
Graves, Tom
    1989   The Elements of Pendulum Dowsing. Shaftesbury, Dorset: Element Books.

Lubek, Walter
    1998   Pendulum Healing Handbook. Twin Lakes, Wisconson: Lotus Light Publications.

Psychic
Browne, Sylvia
    2000   Life on the Other Side. Middlesex, England: Penquin Books.

1999   The Other Side and Back. New York, New York: Penguin Group.

Reed, Henry, McGarey, William A. and Thurston, Mark
1996   Edgar Cayce Guides: Awakening Your Psychic Powers. St. Martin's Paperbacks.

Sanders, Pete A.
1999   You Are Psychic. New York, New York: Fireside

Religion
The Bible – several versions available.

Baigent, Michael; Leigh, Richard and Lincoln, Henry
2005   Holy Blood, Holy Grail Illustrated Edition: The Secret History of Jesus, the Shocking Legacy of the Grail. Delacorte Press.

Brown, Dan
2003   The Da Vinci Code. New York, New York: Doubleday

Gardner, Laurence
2002   Blood Line of the Holy Grail: The Hidden Legacy of Jesus Revealed. Fair Winds Press.

Symbols
Chetwynd, Tom
1982   Dictionary of Symbols. London, Paladin Books: Harper Collins.

Summer Rains, Mary and Greystone, Alex
    1996   Guide to Dream Symbols. Charlotteville, Virginia: Harper Roads Publishing Company.

Tarot

Gray, Eden
    1970   A Complete Guide to the Tarot. New York, New York: Library of Congress.

Waite, A.E.
    2003   The Pictorial Key to the Tarot. Kessinger Publishing.

Wirth, Oswald
    1985   The Tarot of the Magicians. New York, New York: Library of Congress.

Cowie, Norma
    1983   Tarot for Successful Living

General

Becker, Dr. Robert O. and Gary Selden
    1985   The Body Electric. New York: Quill, William Morrow.

Cameron, Julia
    1992   The Artist's Way. New York, New York: Jeremy P. Tarcher/Putnam.

Davidson, Gustav
    1967   Dictionary of Angels. New York, New York: The Free Press.

Emoto, Masaru
    2004   The Hidden Messages in Water. Hillsboro, Oregon: Beyond Words Publications.

Kroeger, Hanna
    1973   The Pendulum, The Bible and Your Survival. Hanna Kroeger Publications.

Morgan, Marlo
    1991   Mutant Message Down Under. New York, New York: Harper Collins.

Redfield, James
    1993   The Celestine Prophecy. New York, New York: Warner Books Inc.

Walsch, Neale Donald
    1996   Conversations With God. New York, New York: G.P. Putnam & Sons.

Appendix II: A Suggested Internet Resources

There are literally millions of sites on the internet. You may do a "search" to give you a list of sites which contain your key words. It is only by visiting them that you will be able to determine which are useful to you. Don't forget that from one site, you can often be directed to related sites.

What follows is simply a sample of Internet Resources. You are encouraged to extend your search on topics of interest to you.

Art & Graphics

www.canva.com

Aura

http://www.bioenergyfields.org/index.asp?secid=3&subsecid=0

World Religions

http://www.mnsu.edu/emuseum/cultural/religion/

http://www.religion-cults.com/

http://en.wikipedia.org/wiki/Major_world_religions

- Islam
  http://images.google.ca/images?svnum=10&hl=en&lr=&q=islam+symbol&btnG=Search
- Christianity
  http://images.google.ca/images?svnum=10&hl=en&lr=&q=christianity+symbol&btnG=Search
- Hinduism
  http://images.google.ca/images?q=Hinduism+symbol&ndsp=20&svnum=10&hl=en&lr=&start=60&sa=N

  http://www.mnsu.edu/emuseum/cultural/religion/hinduism/beliefs.html
- Buddhism
  http://www.mnsu.edu/emuseum/cultural/religion/buddhism/beliefs.html
- Judaism
  http://images.google.ca/images?q=judaism+symbols&ndsp=20&svnum=10&hl=en&lr=&start=40&sa=N
- Traditional Chinese
  http://images.google.ca/images?q=Tao+symbols&ndsp=20&svnum=10&hl=en&lr=&start=80&sa=N
- Bahai faith
  http://images.google.ca/images?svnum=10&hl=en&lr=&q=bahai+faith+symbol&btnG=Search

Ascended Masters

http://www.dci.dk/en/mtrl/saibabaeng.html

http://www.srisathyasai.org.in/Pages/SriSathyaSaiBaba/Introduction.htm

http://www.greatdreams.com/masters/ascended-masters.htm

http://en.wikipedia.org/wiki/Ascended_master#Examples_of_ascended_masters

http://www.theascendedmasters.com/

http://en.wikipedia.org/wiki/Count_of_St_Germain

Kirlian Photography

http://images.google.ca/images?svnum=10&hl=en&lr=&q=kirlian+photography&btnG=Search

Moon
https://www.elitedaily.com/p/the-8-moon-phases-how-they-affect-your-body-mind-2754760

Wikipedia

Appendix III: A Suggested Video Resources

The film industry has released many movies which depict metaphysical beliefs and phenomena; just a few of them are listed here. While they are fantasy, they may improve your understanding of topics addressed in this course.

1999 What Dreams May Come

    Directed by Vincent Ward

1999 The Sixth Sense

    Directed by M. Night Shayamalan

1999 The Matrix

    Directed by Andy Wachowski and Larry Wachowski

1999 Ninth Gate

    Directed by Roman Polanski

1999 Patch Adams

Directed by Tom Shadyac

1996 Michael
Directed by Nora Ephron

1996 Phenomenon
Directed by John Turtletaub

1991 Stigmata
Directed by Rupert Wainright

1990 Ghost
Directed by Jerry Zucker

Appendix IV: A Glossary of Common Terms

Apparitions

Are appearances of ghosts, spirits or bilocation, which can be seen momentarily by human beings.

Apports

Are physical objects materialized through mind energy by beings from the invisible realms. These objects can be given to human beings who may have them in their possession for years as physical objects but the apports may suddenly disappear. These can be objects which have been either brought through psychokinetic energy from other places on the Earth, or which may have been translated from the invisible levels of being.

Ascended Master

An Ascended Master is a being who has become Self-Realized and serves humanity, a being who has raised his/her vibration to a sustained frequency of light. He/she can come and go at will from the Earth plane without the Birth//Death cycle.

Astral Healing

Your spirit travels to do the healing.

Astral Possession or Influence

The experience of an individual being taken over, or influenced by an entity from the astral-mental level of vibration. The possessing entity is usually an Earthbound spirit who has lost contact with the higher aspect of himself. He (or she) is, himself, in need of healing. Striving for attention, some sort of self-expression or power, he is often very coercive toward the human being whom he has taken over. He will order the human to do senseless things, frighten him and otherwise abuse his individual freedom of choice. The difference between astral influence and astral possession is a matter of degree. Influence can be pressed upon an individual from outside his aura, and may be sporadic. In such cases, the individual is said to "act like two persons" or to have a "split personality". In a case of possession, the entity has entered the aura of the human being and has taken over his consciousness. Astral possessions or influence can be healed very simply through techniques of astral healing.

Astral Projection

The ability to send your astral body out into time and travel separate of the physical body.

Belief

A thought accepted as a concept by the subconscious mind. It has become a subconscious attitude toward life, and thus influences the present and future experiences of the individual.

Clairaudience

"Clear hearing"; hearing through the "inner ears" words or ideas from higher vibrational levels, hearing of "etheric music" or the "om" (the basic vibration of the universe), or other sounds of the spiritual universe.

Claircognizance

"Clear Knowing"; the ability to psychically know clearly. (Cognition – the act or faculty of knowing. The product of this act, a perception or insight.)

Clairsentience

"Clear Feeling" (Sentience - Capable of sensation or feeling, conscious or aware of something; for example, sentient beings. From Latin - sentiens from sentire- to feel.)

Clairvoyance

"Clear seeing"; seeing into the higher levels of vibration forms which cannot be seen with the physical eyes, such as visions, auras, energies, or higher beings.

Conditioning

A fixed reaction to an outer stimulus which is crystallized into a pattern of behavior.

Cult

A religion or religious sect generally considered to be extremist or false, with its followers often living in an unconventional manner under the guidance of an authoritarian, charismatic leader.

Dowsing

(Also known as "Witching") A method of divining the location of water or some underground mineral by the use of rods held by a sensitive. Through mind energy the rods are moved in such a way as to indicate the presence of the sought element. This is done under the direction of a "spirit teacher" or "guide" that is channeling information through the mind and body of the sensitive operating the rods.

Dream Analysis

The ability to analyze the symbols that are in your dreams.

(The Field of) Extra Sensory Perception (ESP)

The apparent power to perceive things that are not present to the senses including telepathy, clairvoyance, clairaudience, clairsentience, precognition, psychometry, astral projection, dream analysis, psychic reading, impressions, soul sensing, and communication with animals and other forms of life. ESP may also be called the "spiritual".

Facilitator

Person directing the scan of the subject by the scanner and verbally communicating with any found spirits through the scanner during a session.

Ghosts

A ghost is an Earth-bound individual who has passed over from the physical life into the celestial world through death. Existing at near-physical level of vibration and usually trying to gain the attention of human beings in the physical world. Ghosts need love and healing. Ghosts can be healed through astral healing techniques.

Hallucinations

Are pictures of thoughts and figures from the subconscious mind of an individual which appear to him as real. They are thought forms seen with the "third eye". The person seeing them is really conjuring them up out of his own imagination. He is creating these thought forms as he sees them. Hallucinations are many times the result of distorted mental process.

Hypnosis

Is the induction of a trance state through the use of trance induction technique. The hypnotist leads the subject into hypnosis by causing him to relax his conscious mind and his will. The hypnotist then leads the subconscious mind of the subject through the power of suggestion. Allowing oneself to be hypnotized by another person is not recommended as a way to gain self-authority and self-dominion for it gives to another the power of directly influencing one's subconscious mind. Self-hypnosis does not rob us of our self-authority.

Impressions

The ability to sense vibrations, thought forms and to read them.

Intuition

Intuition is defined as that ability of the mind to develop answers to questions without consciously dealing with the problem at hand. Often a question will provoke your mind to answer without using conscious processing time, and the answer is said to come "out of the blue" or "suddenly, it just struck me." Of all the many abilities of the mind, this is one of the most often used. Just knowing what to do is often an automatic process that occurs without much conscious figuring. Those with stronger intuition make fewer mistakes and can seem luckier, wiser, or more mature.

Karma

The mental register of past experiences, both in present and past lifetimes, which contain error from the past. It includes the memory of cause and effect and judgments of good and evil. It is a law of belief. We are under this law of cause and effect from the past if we believe ourselves to be under it. We can move out from this belief by knowing the truth of our being.

Materializations

Are appearances in the physical world of invisible beings. They have momentarily materialized into forms which can be seen by human beings. This form can be an etheric or a mental body which can be seen clairvoyantly, or a physical body which can be seen and felt physically. Some materializing mediums hold séances in which entities from the mental vibrations appear and speak. These entities wrap themselves in ectoplasm taken from the physical body of the medium, and channel through his subconscious mind to communicate with those who are attending the séance. These appearances are necessarily of the astral-mental level, as the higher Beings have no need to come through human mediums. Spontaneous materialization of Christ and etheric beings happen as spiritual experiences of learning for the persons thus contacted. Spontaneous materialization (higher Beings materializing without the presence of a psychic medium) can also occur when persons who have passed over (through death) into the higher mental realms come back to the physical world for a "visit" for some specific purpose.

Medium

One who acts as a go-between between the spiritual and physical worlds. A medium uses one or more techniques to mediate between the physical human being and the spiritual being or entity.

Mediumship

One who acts as a passive instrument for spirits to communicate with the physical human being.

Mentalism

A doctrine that mind is the true reality and that objects exist only as aspects of the mind's awareness.

Occult

Refers to dealings with spiritual influences, agencies or phenomena, things which are beyond the realm of normal human perception and generally understood to be available only to the initiate.

Paranormal Healing

Is the healing of a physical condition of illness or injury by other than physical means.

Past Life

Relates to reincarnation, the belief that a human being can survive death to be reborn in a new body, bringing with him past integrated experiences.

(The use of) Pendulums:

A technique for learning, in which a pendulum dangling from a cord held by a sensitive, is set into motion by mind energy, channeled through the autonomic nervous system of the sensitive. This channeling may come from different levels of being, such as the level of spirit or of his subconscious mind.

Poltergeist

Or "noisy ghosts" are entities who are caught by mental fascination on the lower astral level of vibration. Having lost communication with their true sense of identity, they exist in a state of childish playfulness. They find great amusement in upsetting physical objects and playing tricks on human beings, but their humor can be malicious. They are in need of healing, and they can be healed through techniques of astral healing.

Precognition

The ability to sense future trends or happenings through the reading of present mental states. This can be done for the self, another individual, a group of people or the whole world.

Projection

As a spontaneous experience, projection is the traveling of an individual, in an inner body, to another place. Sometimes other people can see him there. Projection can occur while the person is either awake or asleep.

Psychic

Capable of extraordinary mental processes, such as extrasensory perception and mental telepathy.

Psychic Readings

The ability to read impressions of the thoughts of another person by sensing the other's mental state. Since present mental states create our future experiences, a "psychic reader" can thus foretell the future and can, by the same process, read the past. It is well to interpolate here that no prediction of the future is final. Changing the present processes can change future trends.

(The Field of) Psychokinesis

The influence of thought on plant growth has been investigated by various scientific and religious groups, and many experiments have proven that positive and negative thought definitely influence the growth of plants.

Psychometry

"Mind measure"- the ability to sense and interpret mental vibrations recorded in a physical object or in a certain place. It may be noted that all the sensing faculties of the astral-mental level register communications from the mind to mind. They may not be reliable, since the mind at this level can be conditioned by false thinking.

Regression

Regression is the process of leading a hypnotized subject backward into past experiences through the power of mental suggestion. The subject becomes able to feel and re-live these experiences. The past experiences can have occurred in either the present or a former lifetime. Regression is sometimes done for the purposes of proving reincarnation or healing past traumas. However, regression is not needed for healing if one understands the principles of scientific prayer.

Reincarnation

Is the return of a soul into the physical world in a new body after the death of one's physical body. A long held concept of reincarnation is that the new incarnation brings back with him or her all of the deep-seated memories of former incarnations, and all of the karmic debts. Thus, the individual comes into the world again with all of the problems which are held over from former lives.

Scanner

A person who is in a hypnotized or mediated state making contact with the subject's energy for the purpose of scanning their emotional, physical, spiritual and mental wellbeing.

Séance

A meeting of people for the purpose of obtaining messages from the spiritual. Usually facilitated by a medium who, with the help of his or her guide, attempts to make contact with a member of the spirit world, be it a deceased friend, family member or famous person. In the past they were sometimes called "circles" because participants, called 'sitters', sat around a table (or on chairs arranged in a circle) in order to link hands, in the belief that this boosted the psychic forces which encourage paranormal manifestations. Since Harry Houdini's death, countless attempts have been made to contact him through séances.

Soul Sensing

The feeling of love and harmony in the soul.

Spiritualism

A religious movement, prominent from the 1840s to the 1920s, found primarily in English-speaking countries. The movement's distinguishing feature is the belief that the spirits of the dead can be contacted by adepts. These spirits are believed to lie on a higher spiritual plane than humans and are therefore capable of providing guidance in both worldly and spiritual matters.

Subconscious Habit

A habit of thinking which has been subjectified. It becomes a habit of thought and emotion, which plays itself again and again, unless it is dissolved by an opposing thought pattern.

Telepathy

"Tele" means "at a distance" and "pathy" means "feeling". Thus, telepathy is the ability to sense thoughts or emotions at a distance. An example of this is when the telephone rings, knowing who is calling and what another person is just about to say.

Teleportation

Is the movement of physical objects by the use of mind energy alone. This is usually done by beings from the invisible realms. Ghosts and poltergeists sometimes move, throw, or drop objects, open or close doors, turn off or on lights, television sets, radios and so on. Higher beings may also do these things for the purpose of communicating or teaching a lesson of Truth.

Web Address:

Art

www.Canva.com

Wikipedia

A Special thank you to my first
Astrology teachers
Phyllis Chubb (Vedic - Eastern) and
Keith Andrews (Western), & Cheryl Forrest, my
first intuitive teacher.

Shift happens...Create magic!
Dream BIGGER!

Constance Santego is a Master Educator and Healer of the Holistic and Spiritual Arts, Author of six books, two of which are series. She is known for bridging the body, mind, and soul consciousness to create your dreams into reality.

Constance's background is in business, owning her first company at the age of twenty-seven until her back went out and she had to sell. Learning to heal herself holistically, she gained many, many certificates and diplomas in spirituality and natural healing from amazing schools around the world.

In 1999, she opened a school that became accredited in the holistic arts and ran that until 2012, teaching students from all over the world how to heal themselves and others.

Constance continually strives to advance her knowledge and is currently in the process of attaining her Ph.D. and DOCTORATE in Natural and Integrative Medicine.

The art of healing seems to open a gate to quantum energy, where magic seems to be taking place. But it must be a science since if I can teach others to do what I can do, it can't be imaginary... and if these teachable spiritual gifts are in the Bible, then it has been taught for over two thousand years.

ALSO AVAILABLE

Play the game Ikona – Discover Your Virtues and Sins

For additional information on

Constance Santego's

wide range of Motivational Products, Coaching Sessions,
Spiritual Retreats,
Live Events and Educational Programs

Go to

www.ConstanceSantego.ca

Follow on Instagram - Constance_Santego &
Facebook - constancesantegoo

Subscribe and receive Free Information and Meditations
on my
YouTube Channel - Constance Santego

www.ingramcontent.com/pod-product-compliance
Lightning Source LLC
Chambersburg PA
CBHW071808080526
44589CB00012B/728